Past Masters
General Editor Keith Thomas

William Morris

Past Masters

AQUINAS Anthony Kenny
ARISTOTLE Jonathan Barnes
FRANCIS BACON Anthony
  Quinton
BAYLE Elisabeth Labrousse
BERKELEY J. O. Urmson
THE BUDDHA Michael Carrithers
BURKE C. B. Macpherson
CARLYLE A. L. Le Quesne
CLAUSEWITZ Michael Howard
COBBETT Raymond Williams
COLERIDGE Richard Holmes
CONFUCIUS Raymond Dawson
DANTE George Holmes
DARWIN Jonathan Howard
DIDEROT Peter France
GEORGE ELIOT Rosemary
  Ashton

ENGELS Terrell Carver
GALILEO Stillman Drake
HEGEL Peter Singer
HOMER Jasper Griffin
HUME A. J. Ayer
JESUS Humphrey Carpenter
KANT Roger Scruton
MACHIAVELLI Quentin Skinner
MARX Peter Singer
MONTAIGNE Peter Burke
THOMAS MORE Anthony Kenny
WILLIAM MORRIS Peter Stansky
MUHAMMAD Michael Cook
NEWMAN Owen Chadwick
PASCAL Alban Krailsheimer
PLATO R. M. Hare
PROUST Derwent May
TOLSTOY Henry Gifford

Forthcoming

AUGUSTINE Henry Chadwick
BACH Denis Arnold
BERGSON Leszek Kolakowski
JOSEPH BUTLER R. G. Frey
CERVANTES P. E. Russell
CHAUCER George Kane
COPERNICUS Owen Gingerich
ERASMUS James McConica
GIBBON J. W. Burrow
GODWIN Alan Ryan
GOETHE T. J. Reed
HERZEN Aileen Kelly
JEFFERSON Jack P. Greene
JOHNSON Pat Rogers
LAMARCK L. J. Jordanova

LEIBNIZ G. M. Ross
LINNAEUS W. T. Stearn
LOCKE John Dunn
MENDEL Vitezslav Orel
MILL William Thomas
NEWTON P. M. Rattansi
ST PAUL G. B. Caird
PETRARCH Nicholas Mann
RUSKIN George P. Landow
SHAKESPEARE Germaine Greer
ADAM SMITH D. D. Raphael
SOCRATES Bernard Williams
SPINOZA Roger Scruton
VICO Peter Burke
and others

Peter Stansky

William Morris

Oxford   New York

OXFORD UNIVERSITY PRESS

1983

Oxford University Press, Walton Street, Oxford OX2 6DP

London Glasgow New York Toronto
Delhi Bombay Calcutta Madras Karachi
Kuala Lumpur Singapore Hong Kong Tokyo
Nairobi Dar es Salaam Cape Town
Melbourne Auckland

and associates in
Beirut Berlin Ibadan Mexico City Nicosia

Oxford is a trade mark of Oxford University Press

British Library Cataloguing in Publication Data

Stansky, Peter
William Morris
1. Morris William - Biography 2. Authors,
English - 19th century - Biography 3. Artists -
England - Biography
I. Title
709'.2'4 PR5083
ISBN 0-19-287572-8
ISBN 0-19-287571-X Pbk

821.85
M 877gs

Library of Congress Cataloging in Publication Data

Stansky, Peter.
  William Morris.
(Past masters)
Bibliography: p.
Includes index.
1. Morris, William, 1834-1896. 2. Authors, English—
19th century—Biography. 3. Artists—England—
Biography. 4. Socialists—England—Biography. I. Title.
II. Series.
PR5083.S7 1983 821'8 [B] 83-4185
ISBN 0-19-287572-8
ISBN 0-19-287571-X (pbk.)

222686

Set by Colset Pte Ltd, Singapore
Printed in Great Britain by
Cox & Wyman Ltd, Reading

Preface

I am grateful to Keith Thomas and Henry Hardy for asking me to write this essay. My debts are many, particularly to those who are expert on William Morris: Chimen Abramsky, Sanford and Helen Berger, Ron Goldstein, Norman Kelvin, and especially Joseph Dunlap. I also wish to thank William Abrahams as well as Barbara Gaerlan, Ann Halsted, Loraine Sinclair, Vanessa Malcarne and Barbara Wawrzynski.

I should like to thank the Society of Antiquaries, London, for permission to quote from the unpublished writings of William Morris.

Stanford University   P. S.

Contents

Abbreviations and note on sources

The following abbreviations are used:

H   Philip Henderson, ed., *The Letters of William Morris to His Family and Friends* (1950).

CW   May Morris, ed., *Collected Works*, 24 volumes (1910–15).

MS   Manuscript, from various manuscript collections including the Beinecke Library, Yale University; the British Library; the Bodleian Library, Oxford; the Berger Collection, Carmel; Columbia University Library; the Huntington Library, San Marino; The National Library of Iceland; the William Morris Gallery, Walthamstow.

The description by Henry James on p. 21 is from his *Letters*, ed. L. Edel, I (1974), 93–4. 'The growth of decorative art . . .' (p. 33) is from P. Henderson, *William Morris* (1967), 66. The interview with Emma Lazarus quoted on p. 36 was published in *The Century Illustrated Monthly Magazine* (July 1886), XXXII, 397. 'As regards colour . . .' on pp. 39–40 is from A. Charles Sewter, *The Stained Glass of William Morris* I (1974), 88–9 (copyright Yale University Press). 'to combine clearness of form . . .' (p. 41) is from B. Fryberger, *Morris & Co* (1971), 29. 'The sources of Morris's manuscripts . . .' (p. 50) is from *William Morris and The Art of the Book* (1976), p. 69. 'To speak quite frankly . . .' (p. 64) and Morris's letter quoted on p. 70 are from J. Bruce Glasier's *William Morris and the Early Days of the Socialist Movement* (1921), 32, 193. The quotation from Morris's diary (pp. 68–9) is from Florence Boos, ed., 'William Morris's Socialist Diary', *History Workshop* 13 (Spring 1982),

44. 'I distinctly . . .' (p. 71) is from R. Page Arnot, *Unpublished Letters of William Morris* (1951), 5. Morris's rediscovered lecture (p. 78) can be found, ed. Paul Meier, in *International Review of Social History* XVI (1971), part 2, 23–4. 'All of the later prose romances . . .' on p. 83 is from Jessie Kocmanová, 'Landscape and Sentiment', *Victorian Poetry* XIII, 3–4 (1975), 117.

to Marina

1 Youth

At the time of William Morris's death in October 1896, his disciple Walter Crane, the artist and illustrator, delivered a short speech about his beloved mentor, in which he mentioned that Morris himself had wondered 'which, of six distinct personalities, he himself really was'. Was he primarily the author, one of the leading poets and prose writers of the day, who might have been Poet Laureate after the death of Tennyson in 1892 – the 'dreamer of dreams' born out of his due time? Or the artist and craftsman who had created designs for wallpaper, stained glass, cloth, tapestries, carpets, which were in his lifetime, and now in ours, amazingly popular? Or the businessman who left an estate of £55,000, quite a hefty sum at the end of the nineteenth century? Or one of the most important printers the world has known, whose Kelmscott Press not only had a considerable influence upon commercial printing, but also fathered the great private press movement of the late nineteenth and early twentieth centuries? Or the ardent socialist, indeed, as he called himself, a communist, who was bent upon a revolutionary transformation of England, and who devoted a great deal of money and energy to that aim? Or was he primarily the private man, full of high spirits and hot temper, married far from happily to a famously beautiful woman, and the father of two daughters?

Of course Morris was all of these individuals, but it is suggestive of the complexity of his life that he could leave his mark in so many areas in a comparatively brief number of years. He had considerable energy and he drove himself relentlessly, doing as many things at once as possible. To him it seemed foolish that anyone shouldn't weave tapestry, compose poetry, and do whatever else at the same time. He appeared to be in robust good health; in fact, his father's side of the family was short-lived and that constitution took its toll upon him. But his doctor is alleged to have said that Morris died from 'being William Morris'.

Morris said on his death-bed that he wished to 'get mumbo-jumbo out of the world'. He wanted to make life simpler and more beautiful, more worth living, and more worthily lived by more people. These ideas tied his life together and solidified his influence.

He was born on 24 March 1834 at Elm House, Clay Hill, Walthamstow, outside London – though the Morrises were originally Welsh – the eldest son and third child of William and Emma Morris. His father was a successful bill broker in the City of London, in effect a banker exchanging money and discounting bills of exchange, at the heart of the burgeoning capitalist system. This might have had an effect on the young Morris: certainly what he was presently to do could not have been more contrary to his father's career. There were numerous younger brothers and sisters, but with the exception of his eldest sister Emma they do not seem to have played much of a role in William's life. He was very close to Emma, who had some of the same drive that he did. She and her husband spent their lives working among the coalminers of Derbyshire. It has been argued that William's deep love for Emma was one cause of his unsatisfactory relations with his wife Jane.

His father died in 1849, when William was eleven, but before that he had made enough to establish the family in grand Victorian comfort. The Morris family might stand for what was happening in England in the nineteenth century in terms of money-making and success. Morris himself would use the organisation and entrepreneurial skills of the Victorian businessman, first to become successful within the bourgeois world and then to turn against it.

His paternal grandfather, the first William Morris, had left Wales for Worcester; the next William Morris moved to London, and when he was sufficiently successful moved out to Elm House in the country. He became even more prosperous through the lucky chance of acquiring 272 Devon Great Consols, shares in a Devonshire copper mine. They came to be worth £200,000 and were the basis of the financial security of the family. When William became twenty-one he acquired an annual income of £900.

The English have a healthy respect for the freedom which money makes possible. Without that secure income Morris probably could not have waited until he was twenty-five before launching his career firmly. (Before that, there were quite a few false though extremely valuable starts.) Ultimately, Morris's aim became to destroy his own class and the economic barriers which divided people in the world. Yet he recognised that it was his strong financial position that allowed him to pursue his interests. As he wrote in 1883:

If I had not been born rich or well-to-do I should have found my position *un*endurable, should have been a mere rebel against what would have seemed to me a system of robbery and injustice . . . The contrasts of rich and poor are unendurable and ought not to be endured by either rich or poor. . . . Such a system can only be destroyed, it seems to me, by the united discontent of numbers; isolated acts of a few persons of the middle and upper classes seeming to me . . . quite powerless against it. (H 176)

The source of the family income remained important to Morris. In 1871 he became one of the directors of the mining company in order to watch over his investment. The reorganisation of his design firm in 1875 was partly a result of the need

3

to be more careful financially at a time when the mine was ceasing to be a source of income. In 1876 he resigned as a director, and as a gesture of release, giving much pleasure to himself, he sat on his top hat.

Ancestry was not of much interest to Morris. Towards the end of his life, he wrote to a correspondent:

I have no ancestors, and don't think I should care if I had; it would be enormous trouble to hunt up photos of myself and this generation of my people. The last generation having [been] recorded (if at all) before the days of photography and after those of art haven't the least interest even to their grandchildren. Besides I don't think I approve of the whole affair. What I offer to the public is my work, I don't want them to know anything else about me. (MS)

He helped one brother out with a job at his factory when he was in financial need, and he kept in very close touch with his mother, writing to her frequently. She died only a few years before he did. He was much involved with his two daughters, the elder of whom, Jenny, had epilepsy, never married and spent most of her life as a recluse. The younger, May, was extremely active in all her father's interests, as a designer, particularly in embroidery, but also very much a participant in his political activities. (She received a testimonial from her fellow members at the Hammersmith Socialist Society at the time of her brief marriage to Halliday Sparling.) May did not have children, and the direct line died out, although there are descendants of the various brothers and sisters. In every sense, Morris's legacy was to the world, although his more immediate estate went to his wife and daughters, and his firm (Morris & Co.) lasted well into the twentieth century.

When William was six the family moved to Woodford Hall, near the Thames in Essex, the grandest house in which they would live, with fifty acres of park and a hundred acres of farm. It subsequently became Mrs Gladstone's Convalescent Home for the Poor, which she founded in the late 1860s in the wake of the cholera epidemic – a pleasing coincidence, for Morris's eventual involvement with politics came about as the result of Gladstone's concern with the Eastern Question, although he turned upon him later.

There was in Morris, even at this tender age, an intense romanticism which lasted through all his life, and finally united with his political idealism – as E. P. Thompson indicated when he entitled his monumental study *William Morris: Romantic to Revolutionary*. But the former was not lost in the latter. Morris had the exuberance and fantasy of a childhood rich in imagination that had been allowed to thrive freely. What was extraordinary about him was that something of it remained with him all his life, in all his work. It was not an unmixed blessing: at times he acted like a spoilt child, would bang his head against the wall, could not react to others with delicacy and mature concern. But in his childhood all was glory, and he took great pleasure in the multiple activities of the country estate. These years at Woodford Hall were richly fulfilling. There was the extended, almost medieval world of Epping Forest at his doorstep, where William could wander about on his pony, at times dressed in a toy suit of armour which had been made for him. He learned to read early and his exhaustive reading of the novels of Sir Walter Scott fed his romantic imagination.

His religious upbringing was somewhat contradictory. He was influenced by the intense religiosity of his mother and his sister Emma, but they pulled in opposite directions – his mother towards the evangelical Low Church, his sister towards high Anglicanism. He called his childhood religion 'rich establishmentarian puritanism'. Morris moved in the Anglo-Catholic direction, and even for some time thought he

would take up a career in the Church. All through his life he
had a sense of religious vocation, a religious dedication to his
task to reform the world. It was this emotional and intellectual
commitment which gave his life its basic consistency – first to
change the world religiously, then secularly. His evolution
followed that of many Victorians, most particularly
Gladstone, who was so important in the origins of his political
activism, and then came to stand for a moderation Morris
could not tolerate.

After his father's death, the family moved again – in
1840 – to the somewhat smaller Water House in Walthamstow (now the William Morris Gallery), where they lived until
1856. Though smaller, it was none the less a considerable
house, still in a comparatively rural part of the world, 'a sub-
urban village', as Morris later described it, 'on the edge of
Epping Forest, and once a pleasant place enough, but now
terribly cocknified and choked up by the jerry building'
(H 184). What he might say of it in our time is hard to imagine,
although Water House itself is now surrounded by a pleasant
if urban park, with ponds and an aviary, providing some relief
from the endless miles of outer London, and the tube stop for
Walthamstow uses a Morris tile as its motif.

Morris's ideas are being re-created in a variety of contradictory images. In 1934, at the centenary of his birth, the
Tory Prime Minister Stanley Baldwin (a nephew of Morris's
greatest friend, Sir Edward Burne-Jones) gave a speech in
Walthamstow celebrating Morris, whom he practically converted into a Tory paternalist: '[He] regarded men and women
around him as that raw material which, if life were long
enough, he might be able to mould and work into something
far happier and better than he saw.' When the Gallery was
opened in 1950, the then Prime Minister, Clement Attlee,
claimed Morris as an ancestor of *his* party, Labour. This was

technically true, of course, but whether Morris would have liked the 'demi-semi Socialism' of the modern Welfare State is another matter. A man who had been virtually a rebel and certainly against authority hence was celebrated by two Prime Ministers, one Tory and the other Labour – and it was the Tory who was practically a relation. In the tradition of the English left, there were backward-looking elements in Morris's thought as well as in his literary and design work. Concerned with the future, he frequently depicted in his poetry and prose a past which provided elements of a better society than that of the present.

A great deal of Morris's education was gained by reading and exploring on his own, but he also had a more formal schooling. At the age of nine he was sent to a preparatory school in Walthamstow as a day boy. Then, at the age of thirteen, he was sent away to a public school. In his case it was Marlborough, one of the up-and-coming new boarding schools founded to serve the ambitions of the middle class to educate their sons appropriately and, it was hoped, in the company of their social superiors. Such schools also catered for the sons of ministers, who generally paid lower fees, and were deemed suitable for those who might be going into the Church. Thomas Arnold had already brought about the reforms designed to educate Christian gentlemen capable of ruling both England and the developing Empire, but Marlborough itself had not yet settled down. It had only been founded in 1843, the school was overcrowded, and was not very well organised. For Morris this was a great boon. He found himself free to wander about the Wiltshire countryside, and fell in love with Savernake Forest, the Downs, and the remains of ancient civilisations, the famous stone circles of Avebury, the Roman villas at Kennet. The area fed his sense of romance more effectively than the school would educate him, but he kept a fond memory of it and of his schoolfellows, whom he had amused by his story-telling. One of them was to read his funeral service.

After Marlborough, he returned to his widowed mother and her many children. The family had been somewhat broken up, not only by the father's death, but also by the marriage of Morris's beloved sister, Emma, to a clergyman, which may have strengthened his own resolve to go into the Church. While at home, he prepared for Oxford and passed the matriculation examination – specifically for Exeter College – in June 1852, although because a place was lacking he did not actually enter until January of the next year. Sitting beside him at the examination was one Edward Jones, the son of a poor Birmingham craftsman who was to be his closest friend, and become known to history as Burne-Jones, the 'Burne' being added later.

Before Morris went off to Oxford to begin the broader adventure of self-discovery, one important non-event, or 'counter-event', in his life should be mentioned. During 1851 he went with his family, as did millions of Britons, to view the Great Exhibition in Paxton's extraordinary Crystal Palace in Hyde Park. That Exhibition boldly demonstrated England's fulfilment of the promise of the Industrial Revolution, and her victory over France in 1815. It asserted England's position as the most powerful country in the world: Morris's mature life would be dedicated to challenging the basis for that assumption. He could hardly have known that in 1851. Yet it is reported that he refused to go into the Exhibition because he hated what he heard of the ugliness and vanity inside.

The theoretical basis of his ideas was a hatred for the mechanical civilisation so clearly celebrated in the useless machine-made curlicues on many of the objects at the Exhibition. Thus, as a very young man, Morris was already making war against the Victorian age. He was similarly disrespectful of matters of state. The next year, in 1852, he refused to attend Wellington's funeral but instead chose to spend the day riding through Epping Forest to see Waltham Abbey.

2 Oxford

Despite the achievements of the Great Exhibition and what it represented, England was still, at mid-century, very much in transition. Many of its institutions maintained their eighteenth-century character, alongside signs of the changes the new age would bring. Oxford was no exception. The expansion and the aggressiveness of the nineteenth century were about to start taking a terrible architectural toll on the city, much to the distress of Morris, who had an intense love for what was left of the medieval town. The very year that he went up to Exeter, the early seventeenth-century chapel of the college was torn down, to be replaced by an impressive if gloomy structure based on the Sainte-Chapelle in Paris. It was designed by Gilbert Scott, who would become Morris's symbol of all that was wrong with nineteenth-century architectural restoration. The building of the new chapel took place while Morris was at Oxford, mostly in 1855; the Victorian passion for 'improvement' disturbed his sleep.

In other ways too Oxford was losing out to the modern world – over the opposition of many in the University, the railway was extended from Didcot to Oxford, a reality of the present and portent of what lay ahead. Morris and Burne-Jones preferred to explore the countryside on horseback, visiting churches which deepened their feeling for the medieval past.

Oxford was in a state of flux, responding to the intellectual currents and excitements going on in the University. The Oxford Movement – that new seriousness about Anglicanism, its past and its current practices – had officially terminated in 1845 with Newman's conversion to Rome; but its effect was still in the atmosphere, tempting Morris and Burne-Jones to follow his example, and reflected in a growth of intellectual commitment on the part of some of the students and dons at the University.

His years at Oxford were extremely important to Morris. He enjoyed himself there in large part, as is generally the case, because of the friends he made. Through Burne-Jones he met a group of Pembroke College undergraduates from Birmingham. They too became friends for life; one of them was the mathematician Charles Faulkner, later a partner in Morris's Firm, and a political follower.

The formal education at Oxford in these years was limited, and Morris was only working for a pass degree. Most of what he learned was from contemporaries. The group adored poetry, most particularly Tennyson's, whose 'The Lady of Shalott' made a strong appeal to Morris's sense of the past. He discovered that he himself could write poetry. In 1856 he started a literary magazine:

About that time being very intimate with other young men of enthusiastic ideas, we got up a monthly paper which lasted (to my cost) for a year; it was called the *Oxford and Cambridge Magazine*, and was very *young* indeed. (H 185)

There were twelve issues, and Morris appeared in ten of them with his first published work, poems, tales and essays.

Like many intellectually inclined undergraduates, Morris and his literary friends were enthusiastic and hopeful of the future. They bewailed the present, scorned their philistine fellow-students and acquired a sentimental place in their hearts for Oxford, misguided though they might believe the beloved institution to be from time to time.

There were other pleasures apart from friendship. Morris's reading had always been extensive, but at university it became

11

voracious and more concentrated, and placed him for life squarely in the tradition of his mentors. Carlyle and Ruskin, who are nowadays mentioned in the same category as himself as critics of nineteenth-century English society, were then of course still comparatively young. Many of Morris's attitudes at that time can be attributed to them, and he continued to revere them both throughout his life – Ruskin more so than Carlyle – even though he came increasingly to differ from the conservative, indeed reactionary, tendencies of their thought. Theirs was another influence which reinforced his medievalism, his conviction that aspects of the world of the past were better than what had replaced them in the world of the present. Eventually, Morris's socialism would lead him to believe that it was possible for the values of the past to come to fruition in a democratic way in the future, but he was not yet politically inclined. Only the premiss for such a conversion was there in his dislike of contemporary civilisation. It was around this time that he and Burne-Jones came to the conclusion that the world of the present was unsatisfactory, that shoddy was king, and that they must engage in a holy war against the age. In Morris's case, the form of that warfare changed over the years, but the objective continued the same.

In Exeter College library there is a miscellany of Morris possessions – spectacles, callipers, pipes, pens, and his copy of Carlyle's *Past and Present*, published in 1855, which argued the virtues of the past over the vices of the present. An even more decisive literary event for him was his reading of John Ruskin's works, which – as he wrote – 'were at the time a sort of revelation to me' (H 185). He had read the two published volumes of Ruskin's *Modern Painters*, but much more significant for Morris was the publication in 1853 of the second volume of *The Stones of Venice*, of which the most important chapter was 'The Nature of Gothic'. As early as

1854 this chapter was printed separately, and perhaps its most famous reprinting was in 1892 by Morris himself, with a preface by him, as the fourth publication of the Kelmscott Press, his great 'typographical adventure' toward the end of his life. Morris remarked of the chapter in the preface that 'in future days it will be considered as one of the very few necessary and inevitable utterances of this century.' In that chapter (and elsewhere) Ruskin advanced the idea which became crucial to Morris's thinking: there was virtue in the lack of perfection or roughness in the Gothic craftsman or sculptor, for it reflected the humanity of the art and the pleasure the maker took in the work. It is easy to sympathise with this protest of Ruskin's against the soulless perfectionism of the machine, but it ultimately led to a difficulty in Morris's own thought, in that many of his repeating designs could in fact be as well or better done through the regularity of machines. Morris, one should emphasise, was never adamantly against machines, but he certainly thought of them as second best. That position can lead, obviously, to archaic and bull-headed attitudes, yet it keeps squarely in mind that it is the human being who counts, both the maker of the object, whether a work of art or anything else, and the user. Just at the moment when the Industrial Revolution appeared to be all-triumphant it was important to these young men, and the many others who read Ruskin, that the price to be paid, and the values that might be endangered, be kept in mind. Ruskin reinforced Morris's belief that medieval society 'allowed the workmen freedom of individual expression' because the 'art of any epoch must of necessity be the expression of its social life.' In Morris's mind, there was in the earlier age the right interplay between the individual and the community. The basic premises of the ideas he would hold throughout his life were taken from Ruskin and Carlyle. Though ultimately he would become far more a figure of the left than these two sages, he never questioned their indictment of the shoddiness of contemporary civilisation, or their insistence upon the importance of joy in labour.

To Ruskin and to Pugin, Morris owed his conception of workmanship, sharing with them a concern with the moral implications of work – that work in and of itself could be either debasing or noble.

Pugin and Ruskin were prophets of the Gothic revival, that belief in Gothic as the only truly Christian architecture, dominant throughout the nineteenth century, not only for churches but for an increasing number of public buildings – indeed for some private buildings as well. For Pugin, and particularly for Ruskin, the Gothic style suggested a philosophy of workmanship. Whether or not the philosophy was an accurate understanding of the Middle Ages is another matter, and not necessarily crucial to its significance for the nineteenth century. Pugin, Ruskin and Morris saw in the style an important statement about workmen in the fourteenth century: their labour was undivided, they were skilled as stonemasons, carvers and so forth rather than specialists on a small aspect of the job who were thereby prevented from having a sense of the total endeavour. These workmen were not mere mechanics, reduced to the level of the modern factory, trapped in an invariable deadening routine.

In 1854, in his first summer vacation Morris visited France. The Gothic cathedrals of Amiens, Beauvais, Chartres and Rouen were revelations to him. The next summer he went to France again, and prepared himself by reading *The Dictionary of French Architecture from the Eleventh to the Sixteenth Centuries* by Viollet-le-Duc, the celebrated restorer, whose most notable achievement, attacked by some, was the rebuilding of Carcassonne. But could this revelation of the

Gothic be put to practical use? The problem of what to do with his life beset him.

In 1855 Morris achieved his majority and now had an income of £900 a year. He, Burne-Jones and their friends were talking more and more of a brotherhood, or a monastery, but less and less did they think of it in religious terms. In 1855, he and Burne-Jones decided that they definitely would not enter the priesthood, but rather dedicate themselves to art. His mother was distressed that Morris had decided to abandon the Church.

He took his pass degree examination in the autumn of 1855. But he remained in Oxford, articling himself in 1856 to one of the most promising architects of the day, the 'great Goth', G. E. Street (whose most famous building, started in 1866, would be the Law Courts in the Strand). Street was ten years older than Morris and had just set up his practice in Oxford in 1852. Morris eventually would have doubts about his master's great work: he realised that Gothic had its limitations as a style of the past used for the present and he was uneasy about building in a historical style. But these thoughts were far in the future. Most of Street's practice was ecclesiastical, building churches, among them some of the finest of the nineteenth century. Most important in terms of Morris's training was Street's belief that the architect must not only design the building but have a practical knowledge of everything that went inside it – ironwork, painting, fabric, stained glass. His influence was incalculable in establishing Morris's future conception of his role.

It was in Street's office that Morris met Philip Webb, the son of an Oxford doctor, three years older than himself. Webb and Burne-Jones were throughout their lives Morris's closest friends, and were deeply involved in all Morris's artistic adventures. Webb who, unlike Burne-Jones, would also follow Morris in his politics was, Morris felt, the best man he had ever known. Both these friends were somewhat less emotional than Morris, less given to sudden rages and impulses. Burne-Jones was the more aesthetic figure, and his painting tended towards the ethereal. Webb was more solid, and although the number of buildings he designed was small, he became a great influence in the architectural community as the century progressed. Morris's actual experience in the nine months that he spent in Street's office was rather limited, most of it devoted to copying a drawing of the doorway of St Augustine's, Canterbury. More important was the visit he paid with Street to the Low Countries in the summer of 1856. These tours abroad each summer while he lived in Oxford broadened his conception of art and architecture, particularly as this was before the days of widespread reproduction of paintings and pictures of buildings.

Working for Street served as an important and thorough introduction to architecture. Dante Gabriel Rossetti and the Pre-Raphaelite circle introduced Morris to the world of painting and London bohemia, along with complications of living and sexuality considerably more intricate than in those jolly youthful times the congenial group of Oxford undergraduates had enjoyed over the past three years. Morris was already on his way to being a multiple artist – plunging into poetry and prose, illumination and embroidery – but the question was where he was to put his greatest emphasis. He was living out the motto he now adopted as his own from the painter Van Eyck's 'Als ich kanne', which Morris rendered in French 'Si je puis' (If I can).

He was also becoming a patron of his new acquaintances. His early purchases included Arthur Hughes's painting *April Love* and, for £40, a small study of a hay field by the Pre-

Raphaelites' master, Ford Madox Brown. His interests were turning towards painting under the influence of Rossetti, to study with whom Burne-Jones had come to London in the spring of 1856, without taking his degree from Oxford.

Rossetti was only six years older than Morris, but in the decade 1850–60 he was at the height of his powers, both as painter and poet. The Pre-Raphaelite Brotherhood, of which he was a founder, had been formed in 1848, that year of revolutions, with Holman Hunt and Millais as its other most prominent members. It was dedicated to the return to an earlier form of Italian painting, truer to nature. Its publication, *The Germ*, issued from January to April 1850, served as a model for the *Oxford and Cambridge Magazine*.

Rossetti and his friends were a heady influence upon Morris during the many weekends he spent down from Oxford in London at this time. In 1856 Rossetti did a sketch of Morris as a model for the head of King David for the Llandaff Cathedral triptych. It reveals a rather beautiful young man, caught in a quiet moment. Rossetti, with his interest in medievalism, and in a brotherhood, was bound to be deeply congenial to Morris and Burne-Jones. He also moved them in an art-for-art's-sake direction. Yet the emphasis on the decorative in his paintings also ultimately acted as an inspiration for Morris to make good design more widely available, through objects rather than through paintings. Aestheticism had a negative political impetus – it was an act of rebellion against an ugly age. It was a comparatively simple matter – although Rossetti himself was quite apolitical – to extend the artistic revolt to encompass political elements. As well as the importance of decoration for its own sake, the Brotherhood had emphasised a belief in the relevance of art to all parts of life. This was a crucial influence upon an impressionable young man. Morris was becoming more and more convinced that being an architect was not the career for him. He gave up his apprenticeship with Street at the end of 1856, and moved to London, first taking rooms with Burne-Jones in Upper Gordon Street in Bloomsbury. Later the two of them moved to Red Lion Square nearby.

Although he was now spending much of his time in London, it is appropriate to consider this period as still part of Morris's student years. His complete independence of the great university city was not assured until his marriage and the building of Red House in 1859. Meanwhile, his primary activity was trying to make himself a painter, under the tutelage of Rossetti. Feeling that no furniture was worthy of the Red Lion flat, he embarked upon the design of a settle. When constructed, it was so mammoth that it had to be hoisted into the building through the windows. This object, in all its magnificence and power, is still to be seen in Red House in Bexleyheath, outside London, although it no longer has Rossetti's painted panels.

These years were also a time of boisterous living. Morris gave up shaving, and developed the bearded look by which he is now remembered. They were young men released from the restraints of university life, and allowed to do what they wished in the metropolis: there were frolics, heavy eating and drinking, noise and enjoyment. There is no indication that Morris took advantage of the *vie de Bohème* for sexual adventures; although he regarded himself as a pagan, there was probably enough residual evangelicalism in his system to prevent that. But he believed in the pleasures of food and drink, and his figure began to fill out. While working on his painting he continued his work and experimentation in embroidery and woodcarving.

Ruskin, who had committed himself as a defender of the Pre-Raphaelites, was a frequent visitor. It was in this year,

1857, that Ruskin moved into politics, with his lecture in Manchester on 'The Political Economy of Art'. These ideas planted seeds in Morris's mind that were to flower twenty years later. Ruskin, as Rossetti and Street had done, reinforced his conception of the artist as necessarily concerned with every part of the arts. Though critical of the age, these men, like Morris himself, were true Victorians with an almost boundless confidence in their ability to master all aspects of their areas of interest.

But despite their omnivorous energy and interests, it was necessary to have a focus, and that had not yet appeared in Morris's thought. He still seemed something of a lightweight (though increasingly corpulent!), swept up in the latest enthusiasm of the moment. This, in 1857, was a project to paint murals in the just completed new Debating Chamber of the Oxford Union, for which the architect was Benjamin Woodward, also the architect of Ruskin's admired Natural History Museum at Oxford. It was Rossetti's idea, and he persuaded Morris, Burne-Jones and other friends to participate in the project. They had a wonderful time, particularly as the Union was paying for their food, lodging and equipment, although they were donating their labour. As Burne-Jones wrote, 'It was blue summer then and always morning and the air sweet and full of bells.' The project was misconceived, first of all because windows in the middle of the areas to be painted meant that glare made everything very difficult to see. The ground for the paintings had not been prepared properly, so that the pictures began to fade almost as soon as done. They can in fact still just be seen in the room, now the Library of the Union. Infra-red photographs make it possible to know what the original paintings looked like. They were taken from legends of King Arthur and the Knights of the Round Table based on Malory's *Morte Darthur*. Seven murals were completed out of the ten proposed; Morris's was 'How Sir Palomydes loved La Belle Iseult with exceeding great love out of measure, and how she loved not him but rather Sir Tristram.' This theme of unrequited love had already figured in his writings and would continue to do so. It was, as we shall see, also a theme in his personal life.

Morris finished his painting early and was able to embark upon a scheme of decoration for the ceiling area above the painting. Ruskin found it too ornate, and Morris's Firm renewed it in 1875 in a more restrained manner; it is now perhaps the most impressive part of the design scheme. He also helped in providing a model for a suit of armour, in having it made, and modelling it for his colleagues; one of the most memorable moments in the whole enterprise was when Morris roared and yelled because he could not open the visor. The helmet and sword are still preserved, and may be seen in the William Morris Gallery in Walthamstow. The spirit of the whole enterprise was high, and did not quite have the solemnity that Max Beerbohm mockingly suggested in his depiction of the event in *Rossetti and His Circle* (1922), in which he had Benjamin Jowett, the famous Master of Balliol, ask of Rossetti 'And what were they going to do with the Grail when they found it, Mr Rossetti?'

Rossetti was central to Morris's life in another way. In an Oxford theatre during this perfect summer – it must have rained sometime – he spotted a 'stunner', as they called beautiful women who caught their fancy. She was Jane Burden, an Oxford girl who, two years later, would become Morris's wife. That she was discovered by Rossetti was crucial – it was almost as if Morris wished to be involved with someone who had the Master's approval. In many ways she was more Rossetti's than Morris's: it now seems certain that they had a long affair while she was married to Morris. Jane Burden sat for Guinevere in Rossetti's contribution to the fiasco of the Oxford murals, and from then on she would be one of his most important models. She was the archetypal Pre-Raphaelite woman, as suggested some twelve years later in a description of her in a letter by Henry James:

she haunts me still. A figure cut out of a missal – out of one of Rossetti's or Hunt's pictures – to say this gives but a faint idea of her, because when such an image puts on flesh and blood, it is an apparition of fearful and wonderful intensity. It's hard to say [whether] she's a grand synthesis of all the pre-Raphaelite pictures ever made – or they a 'keen analysis' of her – whether she's an original or a copy. In either case she is a wonder. Imagine a tall lean woman in a long dress of some dead purple stuff, guiltless of hoops (or of anything else, I should say,) with a mass of crisp black hair heaped into great wavy projections on each of her temples, a thin pale face, a pair of strange sad, deep, dark Swinburnish eyes, with great thick black oblique brows, joined in the middle and tucking themselves away under her hair . . . a long neck, without any collar, and in lieu thereof some dozen strings of outlandish beads – in fine Complete. On the wall was a large nearly full-length portrait of her by Rossetti, so strange and unreal that if you hadn't seen her, you'd pronounce it a distempered vision, but in fact an extremely good likeness. After dinner . . . Morris read us one of his unpublished poems, from the second series of his un-'Earthly Paradise,' and his wife having a bad toothache, lay on the sofa, with her handkerchief to her face . . . this dark silent medieval woman with her medieval toothache. Morris himself is extremely pleasant and quite different from his wife. He impressed me most agreeably. He is short, burly and corpulent, very careless and unfinished in his dress . . . He has a very loud voice and a nervous restless manner and a perfectly unaffected and business-like address.

Even after the happy summer of painting had passed, Morris lingered in Oxford, going down to Red Lion Square frequently, but staying on in the well-known fashion of former students who find it hard to leave their university. But he was also there because of the presence of Jane Burden, who lived in Holywell Street. Practically nothing is known about her background, other than that she was the daughter of a groom. She was, as Henry James and many others have noted, of great beauty, and exactly the sort of beauty desired by the Pre-Raphaelites. On the surface it was certainly a highly unsuitable match for a member of the upper middle classes. Morris's mother was already in quite a state of despair about her eldest son, who had brusquely announced to her his change of career from architect to painter; but he had achieved his majority, his father was long dead, and he had a sizeable personal income which allowed him to do pretty much what he pleased.

Jane became famous for her silences, as Morris did for his noisiness, so that it was hard to estimate her. It appears that she was not much involved in his work, although she was active as an embroiderer in the Firm. She would take little interest in her husband's political activities; on the other hand she did not try to curb him. She was remembered for having tricked George Bernard Shaw, a dedicated vegetarian, into eating a suet pudding, and for suggesting to Cobden-Sanderson, who became the most famous bookbinder of the period, that he take up that skill as no one else did it in the Morris circle. She certainly participated in the life of the family, in bringing up their two daughters, and she spent a great deal of time stretched out on the sofa, not feeling well – in the manner of the time. They would take trips to Italy and Germany with a view to improving her health. In fact, she was probably much stronger physically than Morris, and lived on to 1914. They came greatly to depend upon one another, but it was not a happy marriage: it was a continuing sadness, even tragedy, for one who believed so deeply in human love and the importance and goodness of the animal parts of human life. The difference in social class might have been a source of friction; it is perfectly possible for those of the upper classes who are on the left, particularly in England, to be unable to mix with those from the lower classes, despite their intense desire to do so. Perhaps in this sense the English class system defeated Morris in the end: there may not have been enough mutual interests to sustain the marriage. It wasn't that Jane was stupid. Her letters suggest an intelligent and pleasant woman. But their contrasting temperaments, which might have complemented one another, in fact tended to grate. Jane was calm, and emanated the essence of silence, the passionate quietness caught in Rossetti's many pictures of her, whereas Morris was continually active, and undoubtedly drove her to distraction, although he was certainly as considerate as he could be. His style was hardly gentle, but he devoted much time to worrying about her health, going with her to places where she might feel better, and his letters are marked with this continual concern. For her it was a brilliant match, and she seems to have been happy in its early years. It is not clear exactly what happened to her between their meeting in the summer of 1857, when she was seventeen, and their marriage at the little church of St Michael in the centre of Oxford on 26 April 1859. One wonders if perhaps the time was used for her to receive some further education.

Morris's attitude towards women has come under attack in Anthea Callen's *The Angel in the Studio* (American title: *Women in the Arts and Crafts Movement*), where it is claimed that he was guilty of 'pedestalisation' (the word seems a crime against the English language). He once remarked that women were rather feeble on the artistic side, although excellent in business and mathematics. Women workers did endless and boring tasks of embroidery to produce Morris's designs. But

23

then the men in the shop did boring work as well – though perhaps they were paid better for it. In the context of the time, Morris was certainly far more enlightened than most, and in this perspective it seems harsh to judge him negatively. In *News from Nowhere*, his utopian novel, women perform traditional tasks, but do so from choice. He was not necessarily imaginative in visualising the range of what women might do.

The affair between Rossetti and Jane clearly disturbed Morris. But he does not appear ever to have contemplated divorce or any other drastic action. Rather, when Rossetti and Jane were closest, in the early 1870s, he kept out of their way, and did most of his travelling to Iceland. Morris did have a small circle of women friends, most notably Georgiana Burne-Jones, the wife of his greatest friend. There is no indication that they ever had an affair. He preached the importance of joy and happiness in life and work, yet he in fact failed to have a happy personal life. Rossetti, an Italian, was accustomed to associating with artists' models, women of beauty whom, presumably, he did not expect to be also intellectually stimulating. Jane's other known affair was with Wilfred Scawen Blunt, the eccentric poet, political gadfly and womaniser, who was not looking for women with whom to have permanent relationships. His wife, Lady Anne Blunt, Byron's granddaughter, provided quite enough fire for the married state.

In the mid-1880s Morris wrote an interesting letter to one of his oldest friends, which gives a vivid sense of his attitude to sex.

Copulation is worse than beastly unless it takes place as the outcome of natural desires and kindliness on both sides! So taking place there is even something sacred about it in spite of the grotesquery of the act . . . mere animal on one side, inexplicably mysterious on the other: The decent animalism plus the human kindliness: that would be infinitely better than the present system of venal prostitution which is the meaning of our marriage system on its legal side; though as in other matters, in order to prevent us sinking out of existence, real society asserts itself in the teeth of authority by forming genuine unions of passion and affection . . . The economical freedom of the family would clear away the false sentiment with which we have gilded the chain; but to my mind there would still remain abundance of real sentiment which man has evolved from the mere animal arrangements, and that this would prevent indecencies: though as to the outward form or symbol that it would take I can make no prophecies . . . The couple would be *free* . . . We must not forget that the present iniquity like all iniquities weighs much heavier on the working classes than on us because they are cooped together like fowls going to market. (MS)

The year before his marriage, 1858, saw the publication of Morris's first book of poems, *The Defence of Guenevere and Other Poems*. It was dedicated to Rossetti – 'friend and painter'. Although Rossetti had not yet published much poetry, the Pre-Raphaelites' controversial reputation as painters and, to a degree, as literary figures, may have helped bring about the unenthusiastic reaction to Morris's book of poems. Morris was young and unknown; the book received very few reviews, some favourable, some not, but the unfavourable ones tended to be the more vehement, as in one damning paragraph in the *Spectator* (February 1858):

The Poems of Mr. William Morris chiefly relate to the knights and ladies of King Arthur's time, and nearly all the rest of the pieces belong to the vaguely fabulous age of chivalry; though the author has introduced into his poems touches of what modern research or judgment has shown to be its real coarseness and immorality. To our taste, the style is as bad as bad can be. Mr. Morris imitates little save faults. He combines the mawkish simplicity of the Cockney school with the prosaic baldness of the worst passages of Tennyson, and the occasional obscurity and affectation of plainness that characterise Browning and his followers. Some of the smaller poems are less unpleasing in their manner than the bulk of the book, and a poetical spirit runs through the whole, save where it is unskilfully overlaid. We do not, however, augur much promise from this power; the faults of affectation and bad taste seem too deeply seated.

Although the worst received of all the poetry that Morris wrote, *The Defence of Guenevere* contained his best poems and about half of its contents are probably the most reprinted of his verse. That may in part be due to a change of taste. The long narratives of his later poems, which served as novels for Victorian readers, are no longer in fashion. Few modern readers have the patience to read them. The later poems also lack the intensity of vision of the early ones, of the young man waiting impatiently to be married, as suggested in a few stanzas of 'Praise of My Lady'

> My lady seems of ivory
> Forehead, straight nose, and cheeks that be
>   Hollow'd a little mournfully.
>
> *Beata mea Domina!*
>
> Her full lips made to kiss,
>   Curl'd up and pensive each one is;
>   This makes me faint to stand and see.
>
> *Beata mea Domina!*

The poems are marked by their interest in medieval scenes, their sense of decorativeness, their facing the grimness of medieval life rather than endlessly romanticising it. They surge with erotic energy. This is unusual, for one expects to find Victorian sublimation in poems published in the mid-century, but it is not surprising, considering Morris's youth and his exposure to the bohemianism of Rossetti's life. The story of Guenevere and her adulterous love for Sir Lancelot had a continual fascination for the Victorians, and so did its suggestion that private immorality could bring down the Kingdom, as Guenevere's betrayal of her husband King Arthur contributed to the end of Camelot. Yet Morris presents a sympathetic picture of the Queen.

Undoubtedly, *The Defence* contains the best and most vivid of Morris's shorter poems. But the lack of an enthusiastic response at the time of their publication, and his involvement in a variety of other interests, put a long halt to his poetical career. He returned to writing poetry in 1861, but did not publish any verse again until *The Life and Death of Jason* in 1867.

3 Red House and the Firm

Morris married in Oxford, but his marriage in 1859 brought firmly to an end his Oxford years. From then on he would visit the city only sporadically, most notably in 1883, when he declared himself a socialist in those hallowed halls, much to the indignation of the residents.

He had done a lot for one so young: received his degree, had a brief career in the office of one of the leading architects of the period, become a disciple of one of its most prominent and controversial painters, and completed his one easel painting, 'La Belle Iseult', also known as 'Guinevere', a picture of his wife. (He had difficulty handling the human figure – a metaphor, it might be said, for his personal relations, and it is also ironic that by whatever name the picture is called, it is of an unfaithful wife. It can be seen now in the Tate Gallery.) He had sponsored and financed a literary magazine and published quite a bit of his own work in its pages. He had brought out a book of poems. He had married. The multiplicity of his activities was apparent, but his life as yet had no obvious focus. What was clear was that the cheerful bachelor life of Red Lion Square could not continue: that grander quarters were necessary for the married couple.

The ultimate result was one of the most important buildings of the nineteenth century. The construction of the house was the prelude to what were probably the happiest five years in Morris's life. There were not yet clouds in the relationship between his wife and himself. In 1861 and in 1863 his two daughters, Jane and Mary – commonly called Jenny and May – were born. But where to live? The Morrises had taken up temporary residence in Great Ormond Street. Nearby Morris's friend Philip Webb had his office, and the two dedicated themselves to finding a place to build Morris's dream house. They selected an orchard in Upton, now Bexleyheath, in Kent just outside London. It was there that a house in brick, called Red House because of its colour, was built. The Morrises moved into it at the end of the summer of 1860.

The house has been seen by certain critics as the beginning of modern architecture because of its comparative plainness, and it does have the quality of austerity one associates with Webb, suggesting the start of the attempt to achieve an ahistorical style in his later architecture. It was a two-storey building, L-shaped, with the faint feeling of a monastery about it, almost as if it were part of a cloister. Morris in fact saw it as potentially part of a non-celibate commune which might be expanded. The Burne-Joneses – Edward had married Georgiana MacDonald in 1860 – might come to live with them there. That plan never came to anything. It had been seriously discussed in 1864 but decided against, and Morris's thinking about the house, his attachment to it, is reflected in his reaction to the news: 'As to our palace of Art, I confess your letter was a blow to me at first, but hardly an unexpected one: in short I cried, but I have got over it now' (H 22). Friends came to visit continually, and there were festive times, a continuation of the jolly life of Oxford and Red Lion Square. It was a wonderful place for entertaining and pranks, and the remaining orchard and the imitation medieval garden made the outside attractive as well. The building was not as new in conception as it was sometimes claimed to be. Its elements were based on Webb's experience with Street, the vicarages Street had built, and on Webb's sketches of the work of another prominent Victorian architect, William Butterfield. It was similar to the brick Gothic-style schools that both established architects had built. The building had, however, distinctive touches of pure Webb, removing itself from the fanciness and ornamentation that were hallmarks of Victorian styles of architecture. It also reflected loyalty to local material – brick was much easier to come by in the area than stone.

The house was thought of in a romantic way, appropriately as the first residence of a newly married couple. The interior was not in the light and airy modern style, but was rather dark and medieval, with heavy furnishings. The settle and wardrobe were brought from Red Lion Square, and Webb designed other objects as well – in a plain Gothic style – beds, chairs, candlesticks, glass and so forth. The important point was not that these designs were necessarily revolutionary, but that Morris, Webb and their friends felt that the goods available to be purchased were not satisfactory. One needed to design for oneself. There were murals and hangings on some walls, but most of the walls and ceilings were covered by colourful patterns devised by Morris. Not much notice was paid to the house in the architectural press until towards the end of the century, when Morris and Webb were obviously names to be reckoned with. Yet it will not do to go too far in denying the house its importance. It may not have attracted a great deal of attention at the time that it was built, but its comparative practicality and plainness do suggest what future buildings might aim for: the importance of designing domestic architecture less concerned with impressing others than providing comfort for those who lived there. The ceremonial aspects of an 'important' private residence were dispensed with. The house was not designed for vulgar display of England's riches, but to show that life might be both simple and comfortable (it was, in fact, to Morris's taste, underheated). The ordinary person could not afford to build such a house, but it suggested a direction that domestic architecture might take. It partook of the past in its architectural traditions, but it also had implications for the future of design. Rossetti wrote about the house that 'it is most noble in every way, and more a poem than a house ... but an admirable place to live in too.' Despite its similarities to other architectural developments, Red House pinpoints the attempt to make the smaller house an artistic work of architecture.

It also represented the spirit of Morris's early endeavours – that of a group of friends embarked upon improving the world. With the ingenuousness and arrogance of youth, they now felt they might be able to transform the look of everything about them. What is amazing is how successful they were, despite their many limitations and failures. They showed that serious artists were able to devote their energies to tasks which they might have previously considered beneath them. In this sense, their activities were also part of the professionalisation that was such a hallmark of the later nineteenth century. The issue was tied in with class, whether this was consciously recognised or not. If undoubted gentlemen, bohemian though some of them might be, were involved in matters of manufacture and design, then the pursuits themselves were considered to be at a somewhat higher lever. The class aspects of his activities were not of deep concern to Morris for some years. But from his reading of Ruskin he was aware of the implications of what he was doing.

At Red House, Morris was faced on a much larger scale with a problem he had first confronted in Red Lion Square. In order to find anything with which he was willing to live, he would have to design his own furnishings, or have them designed by Webb and others. With his experience of architecture and painting, and his hobbies of woodcarving and embroidery, he was well equipped to become a designer. But it required the building of Red House – and no doubt the many discussions concerning its planning, and the long wine-soaked evenings spent there by Morris and his friends, to bring about the existence, in April 1861, of Morris, Marshall, Faulkner & Company.

Such design firms had existed before, most notably that formed by Henry Cole, the organiser of the Great Exhibition of 1851 and the inspirer of the Victoria and Albert Museum. There had been a long history of discontent, both unofficially and on the government level, about the state of English design. There was, after all, a great tradition of good eighteenth-century English design. But it had seemed to come apart under the impetus of industrialisation and the development of more modern forms of production. Red House had demonstrated that it was possible for artists to create designs for living; not only unique items, like the murals and individually executed pieces of furniture, but also other objects – table glass, for instance – which might be produced in greater number. Why not embark on such a venture commercially? Related to this idea was the problem that Morris had still not found a specific career for himself. He was now a husband and father, and the Devon Great Consols were showing signs of declining in value. Burne-Jones was launched as a painter, Webb as an architect, but Morris's occupation was still undefined, particularly as his book of poems had not been a notable success.

Those who were to participate in the Firm were Ford Madox Brown, Burne-Jones, Charles Faulkner, Morris, Rossetti, and P. P. Marshall, a surveyor and friend of Madox Brown's. Morris was to receive a salary of £150 as the principal partner, and Faulkner the same sum as bookkeeper. Perhaps Faulkner and Marshall shared the title of the Firm with

Morris because their names would convey the practical aspect of the enterprise better than those of the artists Burne-Jones, Rossetti and Madox Brown. They were all partners with a nominal investment of £1, while the real financial backing, to the tune of £100, came from Morris's mother.

As became a business prospectus, theirs was firmly assertive, and emphasised that these were artists who now condescended to participate in activities such as decoration.

The growth of Decorative Art in this country, owing to the efforts of English Architects, has now reached a point at which it seems desirable that Artists of reputation should devote their time to it. Although no doubt particular instances of success may be cited, still it must be generally felt that attempts of this kind hitherto have been crude and fragmentary. Up to this time, the want of that artistic supervision, which can alone bring about harmony between the various parts of a successful work, has been increased by the necessarily excessive outlay, consequent on taking one individual artist from his pictorial labours. The Artists . . . hope by association to do away with this difficulty. Having among their number men of varied qualifications, they will be able to undertake any species of decoration, mural or otherwise, from pictures, properly so-called, down to the consideration of the smallest work susceptible of art beauty.

The Firm put itself forward to execute mural decoration, carving, stained glass (Burne-Jones was to be the leading designer in this area), metalwork, and furniture. The prospectus also claimed that its work would be 'much less expensive than is generally supposed'. In an autobiographical letter that Morris wrote to Andreas Scheu in 1883, he stated much more succinctly that 'all the minor arts were in a state of complete degradation especially in England, and accordingly in 1861 with the conceited courage of a young man I set myself to reforming all that: and started a sort of firm for producing decorative articles' (H 186). Offices were taken in

Red Lion Square, near the old flat. Until 1865 Morris remained in Red House. When the commuting became too difficult, and after a serious illness, he moved, as did the firm, to Queen Square, near Red Lion Square.

The high tone of the prospectus, common enough in such publications, turned out in this case to be justified by events. Not that the enterprise had a completely smooth history. Morris was a careless businessman, and it was only because there were good business managers that profits were made. Morris was the dominant figure throughout his life, and the Firm continued until 1940, when it went into voluntary liquidation. In 1875 it was reorganised as Morris & Co.; the temperamental painters Rossetti and Madox Brown felt that they had not received adequate compensation, and Morris was estranged from Brown for fifteen years. From 1861 on the Firm was a constant in his life, although undoubtedly he was most involved in it from its founding until he began to become politically active in 1876. During the 1870s he still created more than 600 designs.

Morris as designer had an extremely important practical and intellectual influence. He had a lasting effect upon the look and thought of the contemporary world. Nikolaus Pevsner in *Pioneers of Modern Design* (1936) has argued the crucial influence of Morris for the modern movement, unmodern though much of his work looks to our eyes. He worked in the context of his time; but ever since adolescence, in his refusal to enter the Crystal Palace, in his declaration of holy warfare against the age, he had opposed the fanciness and ostentation of the man-made world – not that all of his own work was totally free of such characteristics. He tried to maintain the Pugin – Ruskin credo of truth to nature and to material and the importance of the quality of workmanship. And he came to advocate a certain proto-functionalism, expressed in his famous dictum: 'Have nothing in your house that you do not know to be useful or believe to be beautiful.' The 'or' is significant, a pure functionalist would argue that it should be 'and' instead. It is also intriguing that he contrasts 'knowing' and 'believing'.

Morris's importance for design has been attacked on two fronts: by those who oppose Pevsner's historicism and his interest in figures in the past, such as Morris, for their contribution to the modern movement and the international style; and by those who see design evolving more by necessity – through the anonymous engineers and others who created what was needed – rather than by any conscious desire to change and simplify. But their arguments in no way invalidate Morris's own role as a highly important and influential designer and teacher. In the early years of the Firm, he was only one of its several designers. But it was he who emerged as the greatest designer of flat patterns of the century.

There was a continual paradox inherent in Morris's career as a businessman. He was not particularly political when he began the Firm, but he was sufficiently Ruskinian to believe that the worker should have joy in his work. While there is no doubt that he enjoyed his own work immensely, it is not clear how much the Firm's hundred or so workers enjoyed theirs. He paid them well, but they were still caught in the commercial system which he abhorred. And though he became more and more radical, he never seems to have felt that he could or should do anything about this situation. Any individual amelioration, he felt, would have no result other than to make his own particular workers more rather than less wedded to the system that should be destroyed. He did not use that as an excuse to treat his workers badly, and he evolved a system of profit-sharing for his senior workers. Quite a few of them followed him politically, although in some cases it might have

been from a sort of loyalty similar to that found in other fac-
tories. But Morris was more aware than he has been given
credit for of the paradoxes of his position, especially after he
became a socialist. As he remarked in 1886 in an interview
with Emma Lazarus, it was

almost impossible to do more than to ensure the *designer* (mostly
myself) some pleasure in his art by getting him to understand the
qualities of the materials and the happy chances of processes. Except
with a small part of the more artistic side of the work, I could not do
anything (or at least but little) to give this pleasure to the workmen,
because I should have had to change their method of work so utterly
that I should have disqualified them from earning their living elsewhere. You see I have got to understand thoroughly the manner of
work under which the art of the Middle Ages was done, and that that
is the *only* manner of work which can turn out popular art, only to
discover that it is impossible to work in that manner in this profit-
grinding society. So on all sides I am driven to revolution as the only
hope, and am growing clearer and clearer on the speedy advent of it
in a very obvious form, though of course I can't give a date for it.

From the very beginning he believed in the importance of
individual craftsmanship. Yet, as Paul Thompson has pointed
out, Morris was no exception to the trend in the industry of his
time *away* from individual craftsmanship. For instance, the
first wallpaper pattern he designed, 'Daisy', in 1862 was ini-
tially produced in his own workshops. But by 1864 that no
longer proved possible and from then on it was manufactured
with other patterns, by the eminent firm of Jeffrey & Co.
Although much of his work continued to be done at the Firm
(stained glass, printed fabrics, weaving, and dyeing), Morris
used machines for the production of furniture, and produced
items in a general and multiple way, not on personal order.

Yet at the same time the work of his Firm was a powerful
influence for change: the growth of 'art' furniture; more

serious thinking as to how an interior should look. Morris was not unique – design was improving in general – but he became the most influential in the field. Even if his practice sometimes contradicted what he preached, his message brought about something approaching a revolution in interior decoration. A comment by the *Spectator* in 1883 suggests the effect of the Firm:

Morris has become a household word for all who wish their material surroundings to be beautiful yet appropriate for homely use, 'neat not gaudy', English in taste, not French . . . Nearly all the better kind of designs in the shops are, as far as they are good, cribs from Morris.

Though its products were generally costly, the Firm did make some simple furniture as well, most notably the inexpensive traditional Sussex chair and the famous 'Morris' reclining chair, which in fact was a traditional design adapted by Webb. Morris himself remarked in his autobiographical letter to Andreas Scheu:

I have had a considerable success even from a commercial side; I believe that if I had yielded on a few points of principle I might have become a positively rich man . . . Almost all the designs we use for surface decoration, wall papers, textiles, and the like, I design myself. I have had to learn the theory and to some extent the practice of weaving, dyeing, and textile printing, all of which I must admit has given me and still gives me a great deal of enjoyment. (H 187)

He could design well because he trained himself thoroughly in the means of production. He had conquered them through his own experience. And his design imagination was prodigious.

The Firm was rapidly successful; as early as 1862 it had a display at the International Exhibition in London. There, the stained glass windows designed by Rossetti were much remarked upon and gained the Firm contracts to provide windows for four new churches built by the architect G. F. Bodley. (Indeed, the windows were so impressive that some thought that they were medieval glass and as such should be disqualified from the exhibition.) The Firm gained its first major secular commissions: to decorate the Green Dining Room for the South Kensington Museum, still in place, and also to do the Armoury and Tapestry rooms in St James's Palace.

Unlike most eminent Victorians, Morris did not appear to worry too much about religion, probably identifying with the paganism of the Germanic tribes; nor were, as far as we know, most of his fellow-designers particularly religious. Yet the backbone of the Firm's work in its early years was stained glass for churches, the result of the great rash of ecclesiastical building in the nineteenth century, the attempt to provide religion for a vastly expanding population, whether it liked it or not. In the early years most of the windows were designed by Rossetti and Brown; later, by Burne-Jones. Morris did 150 designs himself, although he was comparatively weak in creating figures. More than 600 villages, towns and cities in the United Kingdom, as well as a fair number of cities abroad, have stained glass windows by the Firm. Not that all the designs were different. Successful designs were used frequently and the Firm was flexible in dealing with the needs of clients. For instance, for the stained glass window designed for a Unitarian Chapel in Heywood, Lancashire, the figure representing Love is the same as the figure used for Christ in Anglican churches. The commissions were executed through a division of labour in the Firm, with Morris himself being the co-ordinator. Although this ran contrary to Morris's theory of the unity of art, and the ability of all craftsmen to do all work, in fact, as Charles Sewter has pointed out, this was one cause of the great triumph of the Firm's glass, and one reason why its Arts and Crafts successors were less successful. In the figures, most of them designed after 1865 by Burne-Jones, and in the colours, the glass was magnificent.

Sewter has argued that the Firm's glass was the best made since the sixteenth century. He also makes clear how, contrary to most previous practitioners, the Firm liberated itself from medieval prototypes, and created modern glass in a medium which almost inevitably lent itself to a false medievalism. Morris was mainly interested in the qualities from the medieval past which had modern relevance.

As regards colour, where the credit, of course, belongs to Morris himself, no other stained glass of the nineteenth century, or of the previous two hundred years, can for one moment be compared to the splendour of his work in such churches as Bloxham, King's Walden, Lytham, Meole Brace, Staveley, Sunderland, Tadcaster or Tilehurst (to mention only a few), or in the Chapel of Jesus College, Cambridge . . . In his early windows, such as those at the eastern end of St. Michael's, Brighton, Morris's chords of deep green, dull ruby, blue and pale gold have a boldness of contrast and a subtlety of tonal balance which are not only entirely personal, but quite beyond the capacities of any of his competitors . . . [His windows] reveal a feeling for the expressive power of colour which was unique in the nineteenth century, and rare indeed in the whole history of the art . . . At the end of the century a new generation, which owed an enormous debt to Morris's ideas rather than to his example, adopted an attitude which implied some criticism of his practice. The tendency of the Arts and Crafts Movement was to attempt to unite the entire processes of the art, from the manufacture of the glass itself to the completed window, in the hands of a single artist-craftsman . . . The great secret of Morris's success, apart from his own personal gifts as a creative artist, was his respect for the craftsman. 'You whose hands make those things that should be works of art,' he wrote, 'you must be all artists, and good artists too . . . the handicraftsman, left

39

behind by the artist when the arts sundered, must come up with him, must work side by side with him: apart from the difference between a great master and a scholar, apart from the differences of the natural bent of men's minds, which would make one man an imitative, and another an architectural or decorative artist, there should be no difference between those employed on strictly ornamental work; and the body of artists dealing with this should quicken with their art all makers of things into artists also . . .' This is exactly what he had done in Morris & Co.'s stained-glass workshops.

There may have been an inconsistency in the message Morris preached between the claims of the unity of art and the need for a division of labour to achieve the best results. But he was consistent in his respect for the task to be done, and his opposition to a hierarchy among artists. He had equal respect for all labourers who tried to do an honest job. But he came to see clearly that in an industrialised society the commitment of the labourer to his work was becoming more and more perfunctory, and indeed that tasks necessary to earn a wage were increasingly distasteful – that there was a growing gap between work and life. To infuse production with a commitment to art became his way of bridging this gap. From this thinking, one can see why he is, with Marx, one of the greatest diagnosticians of the alienation of labour.

The divisions of labour might make the work tedious, and at times it seemed that women did the most boring work, embroidery and painting tiles, as did Charles Faulkner's sisters Lucy and Kate. Faulkner himself stopped being particularly active in the Firm after the first five years. Morris did not allow stencilling on tiles, each one had to be outlined and then handpainted. Tiles were not a very active or profitable part of the Firm's activities, although later in its history Morris & Co. acted as the agents for the objects made by a friend of Morris's who was probably the greatest English ceramicist of the period, William De Morgan.

The Firm continued its activities all through Morris's life, and beyond, although in the years after his death the furniture tended to be less imaginative, and more imitative of eighteenth-century styles. Still today his wallpapers and chintzes are available, mostly from Sanderson & Co., and are extremely popular. Most, but not all, of the designs for these were by Morris. For instance, in 'Trellis' of 1864, possibly based on the rose trellises at Red House, Philip Webb collaborated with Morris and designed the animals. These early papers had a less intense sense of pattern than the latter ones, which moved towards an increasing complexity and formality. Ultimately in Morris's lifetime the Firm designed 53 papers and 37 chintzes, with several designs used for both.

The aim of textile design, Morris said, was 'to combine clearness of form and firmness of structure with the mystery which comes of abundance and richness of detail'. His patterns drew upon his intense familiarity with nature, and especially with flowers. Later on in his career, his designs became more historical, based on close study of the older textiles acquired by the Victoria and Albert Museum. Morris advised the Museum on purchases, and at times he felt that it existed for his own education and pleasure: 'Perhaps I have used it as much as any man living.' He believed that the designer needed to study both nature and old examples. Fiona Clark in her useful handbook *William Morris Wallpapers and Chintzes* (1973) remarks:

Morris's patterns from 1876 onwards show that this historic knowledge brought increased formality and conventionalisation, and was thus potentially at war with his naturalism, yet in his most characteristic designs he manages to reconcile them. Within a Gothic-derived net of incredible complexity, he combines from two to five different plants without destroying the natural system of growth peculiar to each. These patterns create a 'bower' or 'garden tangle' effect which was what he meant by representing Nature and not merely flowers. It is a synthesis which only Morris, with his sympathy for nature and his degree of identity with medieval art, could have achieved.

Another development for the Firm was tapestry, an art which had not been practised in England to any significant extent for the past hundred years. Characteristically, Morris made the first tapestry for the Firm himself, in 1879. So enamoured of the process was he that he would get up at 5 a.m. in order to weave while, it is said, at the same time composing poetry, finding both pursuits equally easy and pleasurable (it was probably a better way to weave than to write). The result was 'Vine and Acanthus', a study of the two plants with birds, approximately 6 by 8 feet. The colouring was mostly blue, green and light brown, and it is now to be found in Morris's country home, Kelmscott Manor. From then on Morris did the patterns, and the work was done by the Firm. Similarly, he designed most of the patterns for woven fabrics, but they were mostly made by machine, and frequently by other manufacturers. As Marina Vaizey has said, Morris

singlehandedly revived the art of high-warp tapestry, from May to September 1879, spending more than 500 hours at the loom, weaving 'Vine and Acanthus.' He thought tapestry the noblest of the weaving arts, and was defensive about his workers being thought of simply as 'animated machines,' even though their work in carrying out others' designs was in effect mechanical. One of the anomalies is that Morris revived labour-intensive skills, thus pricing much of the Firm's output beyond the range of ordinary people. Yet judicious use of mechanisation ensured that some designs and media had a long life, and repetitions of successful commissions also contributed.

The first major tapestry done by the Firm was *The Adoration of the Magi* for the chapel of Exeter College, Oxford. It was installed in 1890, and became very popular; other versions of it were sold all over England and in Australia, France, Russia and Germany. The compilers of the catalogue of the textile show of Morris work in Birmingham in 1981 state that Morris and Burne-Jones, the two 'old boys' (who had been made Honorary Fellows of the college in 1883) gave the tapestry to Exeter; but correspondence at Exeter reveals some hard bargaining in 1886 between Morris and the Rector, the Revd J. P. Lightfoot, the head of the college. Morris was interested in being co-operative: 'I need hardly say that it would give me much pleasure to do anything for our chapel, and I should be specially pleased to do the piece of tapestry from Burne-Jones designs.' But after that there was some discussion about price. Morris cited 500 guineas as an approximate price; the Rector said the Governing Body had to have a definite figure; Morris guaranteed the price, but reiterated that it was in guineas not pounds – that is, £525. It is an interesting glimpse of Morris, the well-educated businessman, willing to do something for his old Oxford college – very likely it was a generous price he set – but not willing to undervalue the work of his Firm. The college did well, too, for the tapestry is a beautiful one, and is there now for all to see.

In all his design work, Morris believed in trying to be honest to his materials. As he wrote to Emma Lazarus in 1884:

I have tried to produce goods which should be genuine as far as their mere substances are concerned, and should have on that account the primary beauty in them which belongs to naturally treated natural substances; have tried for instance to make woolen substances as woolen as possible, cotton as cottony as possible and so on, have only used the dyes which are natural and simple . . . (MS)

The paradox in Morris's message is that many arts and crafts practitioners followed his theory on the evil of the division of labour and attempted both to design and execute. Morris, after having discovered how to do it, did very little execution himself. He was above all the designer, and his importance as such was recognised in his own time, though he did not call himself a professional, but rather a tradesman.

Because of his reputation, but, more to the point, because of their quality, interest in his designs has probably never been higher than at present, nor reproduction of them more wide-spread. Other aspects of Morris's celebrity have been more volatile. Despite his standing in the decorative arts, Morris in his own time was even more famous as a poet, and eventually more infamous as a political figure.

4 Poetry and early politics

It was in the late 1860s that Morris returned to poetry. His writing would have little to do with the evolving style of his life – in particular, with his efforts to modify contemporary decoration through the activities of the Firm; little, also, to do with the popular Victorian affection for explicit moralising and sentimentality. But it did conform to the Victorian fondness for narrative verse, and it expressed what lay at the bottom of so much of Morris's thinking and creativity: a profound distaste for the age in which he lived.

In 1867 he published *The Life and Death of Jason*, a book-length poem in which the world of ancient Greece provided the setting for a leisurely retelling of the tale of Jason and his quest for the Golden Fleece. This was poetry which did not demand too much of the reader. Its appeal was caught by Henry James, who wrote of it in a review: 'To the jaded intellects of the present moment, distracted with the strife of creeds and the conflict of theories, it opens a glimpse into a world where they will be called upon neither to choose, to criticise, nor to believe, but simply to feel, to look, and to listen.' The book was a considerable success, and it launched the period of Morris's greatest fame within his own lifetime. He had become 'the poet' – so much so that he would be asked to stand in 1877 for the elected position of Professor of Poetry at Oxford, in succession to Matthew Arnold. And in 1892, on the death of Tennyson, only his socialist politics debarred him from being a very strong candidate for Poet Laureate.

A year after *Jason*, in the spring of 1868, he turned from the classical to the medieval world for his most famous poem, *The Earthly Paradise*, which eventually extended itself to four volumes. The structure was simplicity itself. A group of Norse seafarers arrive at an island inhabited by descendants of the ancient Greeks. The two parties are story-tellers in the grand manner, and the poem (or poems) resulting from their exchanges makes up an anthology of tales drawn from the contrasting cultures, rather than a consecutive narrative. It is an immense work that one easily can take up and put down, which perhaps accounts for its immediate contemporary popularity. Thereafter, to the great Victorian verse-reading public, who enjoyed similar poems by the Brownings, Tennyson and others, Morris was 'the author of *The Earthly Paradise*'. Yet the twenty-four long tales that so pleased his first readers are now probably the least read of his major writings. What Henry James saw as the untaxing nature of this verse may account, ironically enough, for its diminished appeal to readers of our own day. Perhaps it all came a bit too easily to Morris, even though he revised extensively. Writing poetry, in his view, demanded little more than the simple skill of the sort he expected from the Firm: 'That talk of inspiration is sheer nonsense, I may tell you that flat, there is no such thing; it is a mere matter of craftsmanship' (MS). But for modern readers, it is the shorter poems, in his early *The Defence of Guenevere*, and the prologues to the various narratives of *The Earthly Paradise*, which are the most memorable and esteemed. These seem almost certainly the result of moments of inspiration, rather than exercises in the craft of verse-making.

As escapism (for it was written in part to take Morris's mind off his marital difficulties), *The Earthly Paradise* was so successful that the Burne-Joneses tended to fall asleep when Morris read the poems aloud to them, despite Georgiana's attempts to keep herself awake with pin-pricks. Perhaps it was legitimate to use the poems in order to escape into the peace of sleep from

> The heavy trouble, the bewildering care
> That weighs us down who live and earn our bread,
> These idle verses have no power to bear; . . .
>
>   and if indeed
> In some old garden thou and I have wrought
> And made fresh flowers spring from hoarded seed,
> And fragrance of old days and deeds have brought
> Back to folk weary; and all was not for nought.
> – No little part it was for me to play –
> The idle singer of an empty day.

The poems were meant to allow their readers to escape from 'greater' London:

> Forget six counties overhung with smoke,
> Forget the snorting steam and piston stroke,
> Forget the spreading of the hideous town;
> Think rather of the pack-horse on the down,
> And dream of London, small and white and clean . . .

Their popularity suggests that they succeeded.

One of the poems in *The Earthly Paradise* series, 'The Lovers of Gudrun', had been partially inspired by Morris's increasing interest in Iceland, the country and its Sagas. He started to learn the language with Eiríkr Magnússon, and became, in this comparatively small area of his activities, as a modern commentator has pointed out, 'the foremost English translator and interpreter of Old Norse literature in the nineteenth century. Between 1869 and 1876 he published an extraordinary quantity of work based on the Scandinavian.' It proved a continuing interest; in the 1890s, he even embarked on editing a Saga Library. It was almost as if the hard and brutal world of the Sagas was a compensation for the softer less demanding poetry of *The Earthly Paradise*, and the later long poem, *Love is Enough, or The Freeing of Pharamond*.

He made memorable trips to Iceland in 1871 and 1873. These journeys, whatever their stimulus to his poetry, were also partly an attempted solution to the difficulties of his married life. Since 1865 Jane Morris and Rossetti had become increasingly close; she was his constant model, and they were lovers. In 1871 the Morrises and Rossetti rented Kelmscott Manor, a farmhouse which had been enlarged in the seventeenth century. Situated on the banks of the Thames, near its source in Oxfordshire, Kelmscott would prove to be Morris's most beloved home. In the first years of the joint tenancy, Morris was frequently away – these were the years of the Iceland journeys – especially when Rossetti was in residence. The arrangement to take the house had been made for the sake of Rossetti's health, so that he might live in the country; presumably it also represented Morris's way of accommodation to the relationship between Rossetti and Jane. Officially Morris was an understanding husband and friend. There can be little question, however, that the strains within his marriage caused him much personal despair. But his beliefs in general and his love for Jane in particular were such that he did not want either to leave her or to deny her wishes, whatever they might be. As for Jane, presumably she did not wish to leave her husband and their daughters for the notoriously unstable Rossetti. So the marriage continued. And the Morrises' relations with Rossetti would more or less end when the Firm was reorganised in 1875.

The trips to Iceland served as more than a way of escape from domestic travail. Morris found there a comparatively primitive world that was far more rewarding to the spirit than 'civilised' England, demonstrating how humankind could do without the advances of the nineteenth century. He found there qualities of endurance and heroism: models for his ideal individuals. It had an immediate effect upon his poetry. As George Bernard Shaw remarked: 'Iceland and the Sagas helped, by changing the facile troubadour of love and beauty into the minstrel of strife and guile, of battle, murder, and death.' Or as Morris said himself, the translations of Norse literature were a 'good corrective to the maundering side of medievalism'. The visits to Iceland impressed him with the native 'worship of courage' and also, as he wrote, when looking back in 1883, 'I learned one lesson there, thoroughly I hope, that the most grinding poverty is a trifling evil compared with the inequality of classes' (H 187).

The early 1870s was a period of trying out new directions. He was in his prime. It was then that G. F. Watts did the portrait, now in the National Portrait Gallery, which is the most familiar image we have of Morris, dark and bearded, with serious and compassionate eyes – a portrait that doesn't quite capture those qualities of restless energy and passion that were so much a part of his nature.

One of Morris's new enterprises at this time was his work as a scribe and a calligrapher. He had experimented in the form earlier, but in the period from 1869 on his activity in this area was prodigious: approximately 1,500 manuscript and decorated pages. Sunday was the day he generally devoted to such work. Probably the most considerable accomplishment in this period was *A Book of Verse* – a selection of his own poems – which he did for Georgiana Burne-Jones. A number of close friends worked on the book – Burne-Jones himself, George Wardle and Fairfax Murray – and the sixty-four pages of the manuscript are marked with an extraordinary freshness and vitality, emphasised by glowing greens.

Morris continued to create manuscript books, of Icelandic Sagas, and several versions of *The Rubaiyat*. As Joseph Dunlap has commented:

The sources of Morris's manuscripts lie in the Middle Ages, the Renaissance, and the fruits of the earth. Whatever he took for his pages – script, decorative motifs, foliage, flowers – he made his own with overflowing originality . . . For half a dozen years he spent long hours of intense artistic creativity with pen and brush which demanded exceptional concentration, clearness of eye, and steadiness of hand.

While he was engaged in this activity, he was very active in translating the Icelandic Sagas. He began in 1870 with his and Eiríkr Magnússon's *The Story of the Volsungs and Niblungs, with Certain Songs from the Elder Edda*, in prose and verse. In 1876, he brought out *Sigurd the Volsung*, which George Bernard Shaw called the greatest epic since Homer, and Paul Thompson in our own time, more cautiously, 'the greatest of all his poems'. *Sigurd* was the Icelandic version of the Nibelungenlied. Wagner had just finished his own operatic version, which Morris disliked intensely. The 1870 publication was a translation – Magnússon probably providing a literal transcription and Morris transforming it into verse, although he himself also knew Icelandic by this time. *Sigurd the Volsung* was Morris's version of the story, his last major long poem before *The Pilgrims of Hope* in 1885. After 1876, he remained active as a writer but, except for the prose romances, his work would now be mostly political and artistic essays, which are among the greatest of his writings.

Morris was deeply opposed to the age, and all that it stood for, even though inevitably he was in many ways a man of his time. But he had not been active in any public sphere; he had devoted himself to being an artist – a designer, a poet. Now that was to change. From 1876 until 1890 the greater part of his energy went into politics.

Morris's entry into the political fray was as one of the crowd. He was swept up, as many were, in Gladstone's great campaign against the Turks on behalf of the 12,000 Bulgarian Christians massacred from April to August 1876. Gladstone was out of office, having retired as Prime Minister in 1874, but with his combination of superb political timing and genuine moral outrage he had captured the public imagination with his famous pamphlet *The Bulgarian Horrors and the Question of the East*, published in September, with its demand that the Turks clear out of the Balkans 'bag and baggage'. From then on, until he was victorious in the General Election of 1880, Gladstone attacked the policy of the Prime Minister, Disraeli, with its emphasis upon 'realistic' politics, and its belief that Turkey needed to be supported so that access to the Mediterranean would not fall into the hands of a major power such as Russia. Disraeli's policy had its greatest triumph at the Congress of Berlin in 1878, but Gladstone won the populace, convincing enough of the voters that moral considerations did count for something in international politics.

In his vigour and morality Morris had certain affinities with Gladstone, and for some years he admired him intensely. He started in politics as a dedicated Gladstonian and joined with other officers of the National Liberal League in sending him a letter of congratulations on his seventieth birthday in 1879. How far Morris had come from that first enthusiasm is shown in a letter in 1885, in which he referred to him as 'that canting old scoundrel' – not, as was true of many on the right, because of Gladstone's growing commitment to Home Rule in Ireland, but because in Morris's view Gladstone's Irish policy was not nearly radical enough. By this time Morris had become a dedicated socialist. The years from 1876 to 1883 marked that progress.

On 26 October 1876 a long letter from him was published in *The Daily News*, attacking in strong and splendidly polemical language the possibility of England going to war on behalf of the Turks: 'Can history show a greater absurdity than this, or greater fools than the English people will be if they do not make it clear to the Ministry and to the Porte [Turkey] that they will wage no war on behalf of the Turks, no war on behalf of thieves and murderers?' (H 83). He threw himself into the agitation with all the considerable energy at his disposal. He was a welcome recruit because of his literary prominence (he had signed the letter 'William Morris, Author of "The Earthly Paradise" '), and also as a successful businessman with some private wealth. He found himself the Treasurer of the Eastern Question Association; some years later he would also be Treasurer of the National Liberal League; later still he would help pay for the publication of *Justice* for the Social Democratic Federation, and then for *Commonweal* for the Socialist League. He turned his poetical skills to the cause, writing in 1878 'Wake, London lads' as a balance to the famous anthem of jingoism 'We don't want to fight, But, by Jingo, if we do . . .'.

Morris's political experience with the Liberals was important in various ways. It acquainted him with politics and political agitation in which he participated vigorously – whatever he did seemed to require of him a maximum of energy. But gradually he began to be disillusioned with traditional politics and started his search for an alternative to the two major parties. This was indicated in a few letters that he wrote to James Bryce, at this time author, academic and young Liberal leader. In March 1877 Morris remarked about the Eastern Question, 'I am disgusted with everyone's conduct in the affair', and then, in another letter, we are now at the mercy of the Tories: if they want war they will have it, nor shall we be able to say one word to stop them: it will be quite impossible to get the working man to the meeting on the subject again. . . . I am sure they [the Tories] will hold meeting after meeting, and triumph, as they well deserve to do. (MS)

The Eastern Question Association and the National Liberal League served their immediate political purpose. The Liberals replaced the Tories in the election of 1880. Gladstone himself was deeply disturbed at how little he was able to do once back in office; he felt that he could not go against the imperatives of English power, at least until he attempted to bring about Irish Home Rule in 1886. But in the early years of his government he found himself forced to apply coercion in Ireland and to bomb Alexandria on behalf of Empire. These actions repelled Morris and helped move him further to the left. He wrote to Richard Cobden's daughter, Jane, thanking her for a copy of John Morley's life of her father: 'I am downhearted at the whole Liberal party turning jingos in the lump . . . How strange that the radicals don't see that all this coercion is one for the Irish, and two for them' (MS).

These political excitements were also accompanied by some domestic upheavals. The needs of the Firm – now reorganised – were considerable, particularly because of the vast increase in dyeing activities based on Morris's experience and experiments with the firm of Sir Thomas Wardle's at Leek in Staffordshire. Morris and his family had left Queen's Square in 1872, and for the next six years lived while in London at Horrington House, now destroyed, in Chiswick High Street. In 1878 he was to acquire from George Macdonald, the poet, novelist and fairy-story writer, The Retreat, on the Upper Mall in Hammersmith, on the Thames. He renamed it Kelmscott House, and there he lived for the rest of his life. Now the headquarters of the William

Morris Society, it is quite a handsome Georgian house, with a splendid location, although the damp from the river is probably very unhealthy. The Firm moved to Merton Abbey in 1881, and from then on both family and business made no further changes: a sale room and accounting office were established on Oxford Street in London, one of the great shopping streets of the metropolis.

In 1877 Morris emerged into the public world again, in a dramatically different way that was significant for his training as a public person and also had a great effect upon the look of our world, almost as – perhaps more – important in that respect than the work of his Firm. This was through the founding of the Society for the Preservation of Ancient Buildings. It was a product of the increased historicism of the period, a growing interest in origins, a belief in a dynamic connection with the past. Antiquarianism was not a new phenomenon: eighteenth-century Englishmen, for example, had been great collectors. The study of history had a great revival towards the end of the nineteenth century, not, as in the past, picking and choosing in order to select those aspects that were particularly attractive but, as Ranke taught, to try to discover what had actually happened. It was saving that record to which Morris's Society was devoted. Virtually the first preservation society, it is the parent of those that are so common today; and the most important beginning to thinking about the environment and its preservation.

Morris had already signed petitions against the ruthless destruction of ancient buildings, but he began to think about doing something more as early as September 1876, when he saw the church at Burford in the Cotswolds being torn down. It is hardly coincidental that this sense of the need for public action should strike him at the same time as he was embarking upon a public role in connection with the Eastern Question.

Earlier in his life he had not been deeply involved with society at large, other than in his private commitment to make war against the age. Before 1876 his warfare had had no public manifestation but had been confined to redesigning Victorian interiors – for those who were better off. Now he was becoming aware of public powers determined to go their own way, to assert the supremacy of a particular conception of English international interests, no matter what the morality of the issues might be. So too economic needs might dictate the destruction of ancient buildings.

There is a political parallel in Morris's attitude towards preservation. When Morris became a socialist, he tended to consider the Liberals more dangerous than the Tories. The latter were easier to fight, for they did not see themselves as attempting to ameliorate the situation. In Morris's view, the preservation movement's real enemies were not those who were out to tear down buildings – although they were bad enough – but those who wished to *restore* buildings, and he drew a crucial distinction between restoration and preservation. The task of the present, Morris felt, was to do the minimum repairs necessary to allow the buildings to survive. Restoration he saw as an arbitrary choice of a particular period in the history of the building – what happened to be fashionable at the moment – and the lavish reproduction and re-creation of the entire building in that style. Whatever was genuine was then practically buried, and much of interest from other periods was likely to be destroyed.

Under the influence of the Cambridge Camden Society, many people believed, for architectural and religious reasons, that as many churches as possible should be restored in the Gothic style. Morris was extremely fond of the Gothic, and adored his master, G. E. Street, one of the 'Great Goths'. But he firmly opposed the re-creation of Gothic architecture which Gilbert Scott seemed to be attempting all over England. Morris launched the attack, and ultimately his Society, by a letter to the *Athenaeum* in March 1877:

My eye just now caught the word 'restoration' in the morning paper, and, on looking closer, I saw that this time it is nothing less than the minster of Tewkesbury that is to be destroyed by Sir Gilbert Scott. Is it altogether too late to do something to save it – it and whatever else of beautiful or historical is still left us on the sites of the ancient buildings we were once so famous for? Would it not be of some use once for all, and with the least possible delay, to set on foot an association for the purposes of watching over and protecting these relics, which, scanty as they are now become, are still wonderful treasures, all the more priceless in this age of the world, when the newly-invented study of living history is the chief joy of so many of our lives? (H 85)

Having launched this idea, Morris panicked slightly and a few days later wrote to the art critic of the *Athenaeum*, F. G. Stephen, 'But now what can be done? The names I could be sure of for a society are but few: but I think we should begin as soon as may be, if the thing is in anyway feasible: meantime I am unskilled in organising this sort of thing' (MS). A little more than a year before he had written to Eiríkr Magnússon 'I was born *not* to be a chairman of anything.' Yet from now on he hardly looked backward. He was exaggerating somewhat – he had tended to be an organiser before, of the *Oxford and Cambridge Magazine*, of the Firm, when he was the figure about whom others congregated. The same was to be true now. As in the fashion of Victorian organisations, a committee of the great and good was set up; the next month the Society, SPAB, was on its way. It quickly acquired the nickname of 'Anti-Scrape' because of its opposition to the methods of restoration, to scraping away the accumulations, the patina, of the past in the service of imitating a particular historical moment. The Society celebrated its hundredth anniversary in 1978, and is going strong.

Morris became secretary of the organisation, and was its vital force, as he was in almost anything with which he was connected. He found himself in a somewhat paradoxical position, having to lend his support for buildings he did not necessarily like. He had no particular fondness for Christopher Wren, whom he saw as the English representative of the hated Renaissance, the period which he regarded as having destroyed artisans and healthy human labour. Nevertheless, when Wren's City churches were threatened he led the campaign on their behalf. Many of the buildings with which the Society was concerned were churches, although as a pagan, Morris personally had little interest in their religious function. The Dean of Canterbury responded to the Society's attack on the planned restoration of the Cathedral with: 'Mr. Morris's Society probably looks on our Cathedral as a place for antiquarian research or for budding architects to learn their art in. We need it for the daily worship of God.' Morris retorted sharply:

For my part remembering well the impression that Canterbury Cathedral made on me when I first stood in it as a little boy, I must needs think that a great building which is obviously venerable and weighty with history is fitter for worship than one turned into a scientific demonstration of what the original architects intended to do. (H 92)

For the same reasons, he now decided, at some loss of business, that the Firm would not put new glass into old churches, but only into newly constructed ones.

The number of cases – some won, some lost – which the Society took under its wing was prodigious. It quickly became

involved in international preservation. There was a campaign
to prevent what Morris regarded as the mindless restoration
of St Mark's in Venice, and for the Baptistry in Ravenna and
the Bargello in Florence. Concerning the Bargello, the
Committee of the Society wrote in 1881, 'The less that can
be done to an ancient building the better: the hope that this
maxim will soon be widely accepted is the very cause and
reason for the existence of the Society.' The campaign for
St Mark's became international, and a considerable number
of petitions on its behalf are still preserved. There was a
meeting at the Sheldonian Theatre in Oxford; the petition
was signed by Gladstone and Disraeli among others. In this
particular case the work had been stopped before the petition
was received by the Italian Minister. Morris was aware that
interfering with projects at home and abroad might be considered tactless, but, he wrote, 'for my part such etiquette
seems to me to belong [to] the class of good manners, which
would forbid us to pull a drowning man out of the water
because we have not been introduced to him' (MS). As he
wrote to Ruskin when asking him to chair a SPAB meeting
'it would be worth the trouble, and years of our little
Society's life, if we could but save one little grey building
in England.' The Society, although it had many defeats, did
much more than save one building. Morris himself derived
invaluable political experience from the public organisation
that the Society required. His annual speeches to the Society
became more and more political, more and more prone to
analyse the arrangements of society, and its past history, as
the cause of the destruction of art that he found in the
present. At the end of the year of the founding of SPAB,
1877, he gave his first two public lectures, one on 4 December
on the Decorative Arts and the second on 19 December, his
first public political speech, on the Eastern Question. They

were the first of hundreds he would make during the rest of his life, the great majority before 1890, when his health began to fail. He spoke on art, on politics, and on the connections between the two.

5 The 1880s

When Morris became involved in the Eastern Question and Anti-Scrape, he could hardly know that at the end of the 1880s he would be perhaps the most prominent figure on the far left in England – a figure referred to in one cartoon as 'The Earthly Paradox'. It was the experience of politics that made him a radical, but throughout his life he had a consistent vision of what an ideal world should be like. He wanted a society which consisted of small semi-independent units, not centrally controlled, but co-operating with one another, in which as much as possible would be done through simple labour, with all members able to discharge the necessary tasks. He suggested that in this way, with the destruction of private ownership and a simpler, less mechanical existence, humankind might be able to lead a better life. In his earlier years, he had hoped that such a society could be achieved through art. Now he came to believe that it was only possible through political means – the achievement of socialism.

In his numerous essays on society and in *News from Nowhere*, which described his vision of the future, Morris was rarely specific about details. What he believed in was the 'religion of Socialism'; it became a faith for him. He was not a good follower, as would become clear in the 1880s, and never formed a successful political organisation, though he tried to. Yet he was one the the great inspirers of the Left in England, and perhaps the leading second-generation Labour Party father figure. He came to believe that socialism would have to come out of the working classes: it could not be imposed upon them from above. That is both his relevance for today and a major reason why Engels attacked him for sentimentalism. He is associated with a socialism highly dangerous to those who have stakes in society, even while he presents an idyllic vision to which many can pay lip service without any fear that it might come into being.

In a famous passage in his 1894 article 'How I Became a Socialist' Morris foretold the dangers of capitalism:

Was it all to end in a counting-house on the top of a cinder-heap, with Podsnap's drawing-room in the offing, and a Whig committee dealing out champagne to the rich and margarine to the poor in such convenient proportions as would make all men contented together, though the pleasure of the eyes was gone from the world, and the place of Homer was to be taken by Huxley? (CW XXIII 280)

This was the culmination of the part of his life that started in the late 1870s. It fitted in with the growth of left-wing activities in England in the 1880s. There was an increased agitation for the franchise, given to urban workers in the Second Reform Act of 1867 and to be given, theoretically, to all males over twenty-one in the Third Reform Act of 1884. A great many were still disfranchised for technical reasons even after that date, but there was virtually no longer any theoretical reason why every male should not have the vote – there was also some agitation for votes for women. Morris himself always had somewhat ambivalent feelings about the whole process of traditional politics. His opinion of Parliament is demonstrated in *News from Nowhere,* where the disused Houses of Parliament are a store-house for manure. He felt that the compromises necessary in a parliamentary system might delay the advent of the new society. On the other hand, he recognised the value of the political experience and was unsympathetic to what he regarded as the totally nihilistic attitude and actions of the anarchists. He was humanly inconsistent in that when arguing with parliamentarians, he veered in an anarchist direction, and when disputing with anarchists he tended to be somewhat sympathetic towards traditional political measures.

The economic situation also intensified the politics of the 1880s. Historians have extensively debated the nature of the so-called 'Great Depression' starting in 1876, but even if it were far less serious than has previously been thought, England still felt beleaguered and was aware that Germany and the United States were threatening her dominion, particularly in the industrial sphere. Though it was the centre of the greatest empire the world had ever known, and, supported by financial capitalism, the most powerful country in the world until the First World War, the poverty of many in the nation became even more evident during this period of economic difficulty. Morris was not the only member of the middle classes who felt that something needed to be done about the situation. There was an outpouring of intellectual talent into movements dedicated to changing English society, of which one of the most prominent was the Fabians, founded in 1884. Although he maintained good relations with the leading Fabian, George Bernard Shaw (who appeared at one point on the verge of marrying Morris's daughter May), Morris disliked their dry unsentimental approach.

The 1880s were the great period of the growth of unionism. The end of the decade saw the Matchgirls' Strike, the Gasworkers' Strike, and finally the great Dock Strike of 1889. Morris himself, although he was firmly convinced of the exploitation of the proletariat, the workforce created by needs of capitalism, and the workers' need to take action, did not appear to be particularly interested in unionism as a means to bring about the changes he wished for society. His style was to be involved in the organisation of demonstrations and personal preaching, which he did every Sunday by

Hammersmith Bridge. His hope was to help foment a rising of the workers: 'Educate, Agitate, Organise', as is inscribed on the Social Democratic Federation's membership card, which he designed. The unions of skilled workers were threatened in the worsening economic and political atmosphere of the end of the century; this led to a coming together of political organisations, such as the Democratic Federation, the Fabians and others, with the unions in 1893 to form the Independent Labour Party – the ancestor of the Labour Party. For Morris, such an approach meant too much co-operation with a system which he regarded as corrupt. As Trevor Lloyd has remarked, 'Socialism in England passed from the age of lonely individual genius to that of organisation and compromise.'

The first vehicle for Morris's socialism was the Democratic Federation, founded by H. M. Hyndman, a rich stockbroker, who never gave up his frock coat and top hat. (Morris, in contrast, wore simple clothes, a smock at work and a rough serge suit with a blue worker's shirt most of the rest of the time.) The Federation became Marxist in 1883 and added 'Social' to its title.

Morris too became a Marxist, though he never called himself one. He accepted Marx's analysis of society, the materialistic interpretation of history and the necessity of eliminating private property. Under the influence of Marx's thought he recognised the necessity of the machine for freeing the workers from 'Useless Toil'; and he came to excuse his failure to provide his workers with enough pleasure by way of his Marxist belief that the individual effort of changing one's own practice would not really hasten the transformation of society. (And a drastic change within the Firm itself would have deprived Morris of the wherewithal to fight the good fight.) Yet he felt that the worker should be neither a slave of the machine nor a machine himself. His was a Marxism infused with his own insights and beliefs, with English individualism and a great regard for humane values, consistent with the writing of the young Marx (which of course he did not know). *Das Kapital* was not yet available in English, and Morris did not read German, but in 1883 he was reading it in French. He made a few famous remarks denigrating his ability to understand economics, which have provided evidence for those who wish to see his socialism as not particularly theoretical or Marxist. J. Bruce Glasier, the Scottish socialist and later theosophist and disciple of Morris, who wished to capture Morris firmly for the tradition of English ethical socialism, quotes him as saying,

To speak quite frankly, I do not know what Marx's theory of value is, and I'm damned if I want to know . . . I have tried to understand Marx's theory, but political economy is not my line, and much of it appears to me to be dreary rubbish. But I am, I hope, a Socialist none the less. It is enough political economy for me to know that the idle class is rich and the working class is poor, and that the rich are rich because they rob the poor. That I know because I see it with my eyes. I need read no books to convince me of it.

Undoubtedly, the major impetus behind his socialism, as it generally is, was moral.

Morris was not totally unrealistic about what might be achieved. In famous lines from *The Dream of John Ball* he spoke of 'How men fight and lose the battle, and the thing they fought for comes about in spite of their defeat, and when it comes turns out not to be what they meant, and other men have to fight for what they meant under another name.' Certainly the welfare states of most of the Western world would have seemed to most of the socialists of the later nineteenth century a very heaven, at least in conception, but we can see how far they are from the spirit of what they – and particularly Morris – had wished.

Morris came to socialism through art, which, Ruskin had argued, seemed to be sickening in nineteenth-century England. He was convinced that art could not flourish in a society of 'commercialism and profit mongering', but there is of course hardly an absolute guarantee that, if human beings turn from thinking only of profits, art will automatically flourish. A series of lectures that he gave on art in the years between 1877 and 1883 charted his progress towards socialism. Morris announced his conversion in his talk on 'Art Under Plutocracy' at Oxford in November 1883, with John Ruskin in the chair, and much to the dismay of the University authorities. He had warned the organisers of the Oxford Liberal Club that he would be taking up Hyndman's position – he had joined the Democratic Federation the previous January – but that had not deterred the sponsors. In 1882 a collection of five of his lectures was published, with the characteristically ambivalent Morrisian title, *Hopes and Fears for Art*. These were the prelude to the public declaration of his socialism. 'I not only admit, but declare, and think it most important to declare, that so long as the system of competition in the production and exchange of the means of life goes on, the degradation of the arts will go on.'

In his first political incarnation he had been a radical, on the left of the Liberal Party, as was evident in a letter he wrote to George Howard, later Earl of Carlisle, a radical political associate, an artist, and a patron of the Firm. Howard had been elected to Parliament by a tiny margin, and Morris wrote to him, 'Here is a scratch of the pen from a somewhat downtrodden radical to congratulate you very heartily on defeating the enemy in East Cumberland. Keep it a-going and before long, please give us radicals something more to rejoice in, that we may be enthusiastic (and numerous) at the poll next General Election' (MS). But he wrote about the Liberal Party some years later:

A nondescript and flaccid creation of bourgeois supremacy, a party without principles or definition, but a thoroughly adequate expression of English middle-class hypocrisy, cowardice, and short-sightedness, engrossed the whole of the political progressive movement in England, and dragged the working-classes along with it, blind as they were to their own interests and solidarity of labour. (CW XXIII 71–2)

Prompted either by Marx or his own rather choleric temper, or by both, he was capable of a certain glorious invective.

As he became more and more politically involved, he also became more and more disillusioned with traditional politics; the logical consequence was to join the one society at the time that professed socialism: the Democratic Federation. He now wrote to William Allingham, the poet:

Yes, I am a rebel and even more of a rebel than some of my coadjutors know perhaps. Certainly in some way or other this present society, or age of shoddy, is doomed to fall: nor can I see anything ahead of it as an organisation save Socialism: meantime as to present parties I say: damn Tweedle-dum and blast Tweedle-dee. (H 170)

He was a considerable recruit to the fledgling party. In May 1883 he became a member of its executive committee. The organisation itself remained small, comprised mostly of Londoners, numbering throughout the 1880s around 600. It persisted, however, and membership reached a total in 1897 of 3,250 members. For a brief period it met his aims.

In June 1883 Morris wrote to C. E. Maurice, a son of the well-known radical theologian, F. D. Maurice:

I so much desire to convert all disinterested people of good will to what I should call active and general Socialism . . . For my part I used to think that one might further real Socialistic progress by doing what one could on the lines of ordinary middle-class Radicalism . . . in fact . . . Radicalism is made for and by the middle classes and will always be under the control of rich capitalists: they will have no objection to its *political* development, if they think they can stop it there; but as to real social changes, they will not allow them if they can help it . . . I believe that Socialism is advancing, and will advance more and more as education spreads, and so believing, find my duty clear to do my best to further it advance . . . A word about the Democratic Federation: as far as I know it is the only active Socialist organisation in England; . . . therefore I found myself bound to join it. (H 173–4)

The difficulty for Morris was that he was not an organisation man, and in any case Hyndman was difficult to deal with. The Democratic Federation, though small, was beginning to galvanise socialist feelings in England. It was intended, at least in theory, to build Jerusalem in England's green and pleasant land. Hyndman was ambitious and determined to have things his own way. He was anxious to move the Federation towards participation in politics, to achieve position and power in a traditional English way. Morris was opposed to this, but not as opposed to it as others were. As Paul Thompson has pointed out, Morris's classic dilemma was that he was torn between purism and practical agitation. As is evident in his attitude to anarchism, he would move in one direction when those he was with tended to move in the other. The official Marxist position as represented by new recruits to the Federation, Marx's daughter, Eleanor, and her lover, the unscrupulous Edward Aveling, was against Hyndman's line. Morris with his supporters – who may have used him as something of a figurehead – acquired a majority on the Council against Hyndman. Rather than staying in the Federation and engaging in further wrangles on tactics, they left the organisation at the end of 1884 and formed a new group: the Socialist League. Morris was to be its leader until 1890. Its membership card, devised by Walter Crane, depicted Morris as a blacksmith at an anvil. Unlike the Federation, it did not try to elect members to Parliament;

rather, with varying degrees of success, to educate, organise and agitate.

The Socialist League was in many ways the high point of Morris's political life. It was not big; it had approximately 700 members in 1886, with eighteen branches. There was a sense of comradeship in it. Morris had written in *The Dream of John Ball*: 'Fellowship is heaven, and lack of fellowship is hell: fellowship is life and the lack of fellowship is death'; in many ways he was a lonely man, particularly in his marriage, and despite close friendships with the friends of his youth. There was an unsatisfied yearning within him for a wider community, and the Socialist League for a while satisfied it. For the first few years, he really thought that it would bring about a transformation of society, the creation of an ideal socialist state in England.

Morris hoped that the Socialist League would be capable of a proper course veering neither towards Parliament nor anarchism. He also wanted the League to support not state socialism, which he saw as the aim of the Social Democratic Federation and of the Fabians, but rather revolutionary socialism. The manifesto of the League stated:

The dominant classes are uneasy, anxious, touched in conscience, even, as to the condition of those they govern; the markets of the world are being competed for with an eagerness never before known; every thing points to the fact that the great commercial system is becoming unmanageable, and is slipping from the grasp of the present rulers.

In the report of its 4th annual meeting in 1888 the League offered to provide fifteen lecturers, who would speak without charge in London, and for expenses elsewhere. These included Morris, with talks on such topics as 'Work as it is and it might be' and 'How we live and how we might live.' He was not a particularly good speaker, as he realised himself. He wrote in his diary about a speech he gave on the Paris Commune in 1887, 'I spoke last and, to my great vexation and shame, *very* badly; fortunately I was hoarse, and so I hope they took that for an excuse; thought it wasn't the reason; which was that I tried to be literary and original and so paid for my egotism.' He tended not to be able to wander too far away from his notes. At the beginning of *News from Nowhere*, he presents a rather dispirited picture of what the worst sort of meeting must have been like: 'There were six persons present, and consequently six sections of the party were represented.' The League was able to do some effective work for the cause of socialism, but there was much internecine disputing. Morris tried to maintain a position in the middle. It was difficult, although he was able to last it out for five years.

In the first years Morris was full of hope. He felt that the revolution was around the corner; the workers could bring it about. These hopes came to an end on Bloody Sunday, 13 November 1887, when thousands of socialists, radicals and Irish involved in a demonstration were dispersed and beaten back by the police using batons. A radical member of Parliament, R. Cunninghame Graham, and John Burns, a Labour leader, were arrested, and sentenced the following January to six weeks in prison. Others, who chose to be dealt with immediately, received longer sentences. More than one hundred were wounded, and two died of injuries. Bloody Sunday ended for a long time this sort of action, and the ban on demonstrations was not lifted until 1892.

Originally Morris had felt that a controlled attack by the workers might succeed. On 10 February 1886, he wrote: 'I look at it as a mistake to go in for a policy of riot, all the more as I feel pretty certain that the Socialists will one day have to fight seriously . . . [Yet] any opposition to law and order in the streets is of use to us, *if the price of it is not too high*. . . . An English mob is always brutal at any rate till it rises to heroism.' Bloody Sunday demonstrated to Morris that the revolution would require force, violence and organisation, the people in arms. The powers of repression were not going to give up easily. (In fact, the Commissioner of Police, Sir Charles Warren and the Home Secretary, Matthews, were much criticised on all sides for their mishandling of the event.) On 20 November the funeral took place of Alfred Linnel, one of the two who had died of their injuries; 120,000 participated, and Morris wrote his 'A Death Song', sold as a benefit for Linnel's children:

> Here lies the sign that we shall break out of prison;
> Amidst the storm he won a prisoner's rest:
> But in the cloudy dawn the sun arisen
> Brings us our day of work to win the best.
> Not one, not one, nor thousands must they slay,
> But one and all if they would dusk the day.

The events of Bloody Sunday intensified the splits within the League over the issue of parliamentary participation, and in this instance the offical Marxists – Eleanor and Aveling – were in favour of running candidates. Their branch, the Bloomsbury one, disaffiliated. Morris expressed his views in a letter in May 1888, to Glasier:

We should treat Parliament as a representative of the enemy . . . We might for some definite purpose be forced to send members to Parliament *as rebels* . . . but under no circumstances to help to carry on their Government of the country . . . and therefore we ought not to put forward palliative measures to be carried through Parliament, for that would be helping them to govern us.

He saw such activities as working towards state socialism, which he opposed. He planned to leave the League if the resolution to put up a parliamentary candidate was carried.

Despite his growing worry about the course politics were taking, he continued to be active. Although he was not sure when the revolution would take place, he never lost faith that it must. He supported the League and *Commonweal* to the extent of £500 a year – 2,000 copies of the paper were printed – and he continued to edit it weekly. In 1889 he attended the organisation meeting of the 2nd International in Paris and was at the Marxist congress there rather than the more moderate socialist one. The same year he declared himself a communist.

The secession of the parliamentary group from the League left Morris vulnerable to the machinations of the anarchists. Perhaps because of his romanticism, Morris tended at first to find them more attractive as individuals than the parliamentarians. He had written as early as May 1887, 'I distinctly disagree with the Anarchist principle, much as I sympathize with many of the anarchists personally, and although I have an Englishman's wholesome horror of government interference and centralisation which some of our friends who are built on the German pattern are not quite enough afraid of I think.' But by 1889 he was less tolerant, as indicated in a letter to Glasier: 'I believe there will be an attempt to get on the Council a majority of stupid nobbedehays [*sic*] who call themselves anarchists and *are* fools, and to oust Kitz from the secretaryship as he forsooth is not advanced enough for them. If this were to succeed, it would break up the League' (MS). In fact, the anarchists succeeded in taking over the League. Morris put up with it for a brief time, but in November 1890 he withdrew, and converted the Hammersmith branch of the League into the Hammersmith Socialist Society. It continued to meet in the small building next to Kelmscott House and to be active for the rest of Morris's life. The dream of achieving a revolution was still real to him. England would undergo a socialist transformation into a country where classes and private property were abolished, where the worker would enjoy his work and the fruits of his labour, where exploitation would no longer take place, where Morris's moral criticisms of society would be answered – but he no longer thought that all this would happen in the immediate future. That is far different from saying that he abandoned that vision; it was continually put forth at the many meetings of the Hammersmith Socialist Society.

Alongside his whirlwind political activity, and in spite of its considerable demands on his time, he continued his work with the Firm. He had a growing influence upon an increasing number of individuals coming to the forefront in design. In 1882 the Century Guild was established. Its exciting new designs were a combination of styleless solidity and an anticipation of *art nouveau* whip-lash line. In 1884 the Art Workers' Guild was established by young architects and designers, most of whom agreed with Morris that the look of the world about them was not satisfactory. The extent of his influence is testified to by the fact that his bust still has pride of place in the meeting room of the Guild. These were not quite the guilds of medieval times. These Art 'workers', who tended frequently to be from the middle class, were important in helping to redesign the world and in carrying Morris's design influence forward to the modern movement. In 1888, the great year for such organisations, the National Association for the Advancement of Art and Its Application to Industry was established. Although it saw itself as comparable to the British Association for the Advancement of Science, it had a brief life of only three years. The same year, 1888, the Arts & Crafts Exhibition Society was founded, introducing that term – so intimately associated with Morris – to the world. Also in 1888 C. R. Ashbee set up the School and Guild of Handicraft. All these organisations sought Morris's blessing and help, and he gave generously of his time if in a somewhat grudging spirit. He regarded them as palliatives, not getting to the heart of economics and politics. Even so, he felt that they were moving in the right direction: their attention to the 'lesser' arts was undermining what Morris and his disciples regarded as the illegitimate domination of the 'finer' arts. Some of these figures followed Morris politically and agreed with him that art could not be truly liberated, be truly fit and proper, until it functioned in a totally different political system.

As Morris's health began to fail, he became less politically active. Despite his having sometimes advocated what might almost be called a simple 'machine for living' – one large whitewashed room which would serve as bedroom, living-room and study, he continued to live in his comparatively large houses, spending as much time as he could at his beloved Kelmscott Manor, fishing in the Thames.

6 Last years

Morris regarded as the two most beautiful objects in the world a good building and a good book. He had devoted his professional life to making the contents of buildings much more attractive. But in his last years much of Morris's energy went into new bursts of activity: into writing prose romances, into book collecting, and into the Kelmscott Press.

He had never stopped writing. In the mid-1880s he had published a long poem, *The Pilgrims of Hope*, about a romantic triangle (similar to his own with Jane and Rossetti) and the involvement of the three in the Paris Commune, which he saw as a socialist ideal. The poem described a conversion experience to socialism in religious terms, a 'new birth'. It had run as a serial in *Commonweal* from April 1885 to June 1886. His next major work was *A Dream of John Ball*, published in *Commonweal* in 1886 and 1887 and brought out as a book in 1888. In it the narrator is transported back to 1381 to Kent and tells of his meeting with John Ball, the rebel priest, who was one of the leaders in Wat Tyler's rebellion. It had as its frontispiece a wood-engraving by Burne-Jones, who continued working closely with Morris, even though he had little interest in his politics. The picture depicts Adam and Eve and their children, with the remark, attributed to John Ball: 'When Adam delved and Eve span who was then the gentleman?' That slogan summons up so much of Morris's socialism: its intense moral character, its characteristic English tendency to look backwards for a golden age.

Morris's most important writing in this period, and the most important of all his literary works, was *News from*

Nowhere, which appeared as instalments in *Commonweal* in 1890 and then in a revised version, published in 1891. It is a summation of all Morris's social values; its vision represents his hopes for England and for the rest of the world.

The book had one of its origins in two boat trips Morris made, first in August 1880, and then the following summer, from Kelmscott House at Hammersmith in London to Kelmscott Manor. That journey, from urban to rural England, from discontent to content, makes up the last third of the book. It is set in the future, and its earlier part is a description and discussion of what England had become. In the *Commonweal* version of the story, the revolution is supposed to have taken place in the early twentieth century. Only a year later, Morris had become more pessimistic, and in the book version the revolution is placed in 1952. The immediate impetus for the book was the publication of Edward Bellamy's *Looking Backwards*, presenting a utopia of Boston in the year 2000 which Morris found horribly mechanistic; he called it a 'cockney paradise'. Similarly, he was distressed by the *Fabian Essays*, published in 1889 and advocating, he thought, a state where the numerous vices of want, the evils of a capitalistic society, might well be taken care of, but where there would be none of the internal values which a new society needed to provide.

News from Nowhere – 'nowhere' of course translates 'utopia' – uses a common convention for utopias, which is also a variant on the framework of *A Dream of John Ball*. The Dreamer of that book becomes the Guest. Rather than moving back into the past, he wakes up in the future, still in his house, but it has now become a hostel and is next to a Thames that is no longer polluted and is full of salmon. (Salmon, one notes in passing, have begun to return to the Thames, which indicates that perhaps some environmental progress has been made.)

The subtitle of the book is *An Epoch of Rest*. The Guest finds a society in which history has stopped. Law courts and prisons have been abolished. A central government has been replaced by direct, participatory democracy, a series of self-governing communes in communication with one another. Small is beautiful, in terms of government and of the economy.

Until fairly recently, such an approach to modern Western society appeared to be hopelessly romantic. But the popularity of Morris's vision has increased since the 1960s, when it became obvious that centralisation, 'big government' and state socialism were not working, that they were failing to provide continued prosperity, not to mention more intellectual and emotional satisfactions. This accounted for the move, in the 1960s and early 1970s, towards communes, whose members – so-called hippies or flower-children – often wore a rather Pre-Raphaelite, semi-medieval sort of dress. The lack of realism in Morris's vision of utopia is not so much in the sort of economy he depicts as in one of his basic premisses: that humans need not be aggressive. The reason why most communes have not been able to survive is that human beings are not sufficiently able to maintain peaceful relations with one another. For Morris, the perversion of human character brought about by capitalism means that humans are alienated from themselves, others, their work and their environment. He may be right, but unfortunately there has not been a society yet, no matter what it may call itself, able to solve the problems of the aggressive manifestations of human nature.

In *News from Nowhere* Morris worked out his conception of how the new society could have come into being. Convinced by this time that peaceful evolution was not possible, he assumed in the book that there had been two years of warfare, brought about by conflict between capitalists – threatened by continual economic crises – and organised labour. He now felt that such a struggle was bound to come. He had written in 1885, 'The class struggle is really the only lever for bringing about the change. Of course you understand that though I would not shrink from a civil war if that be the only necessary means, I would do all I could to avoid it '(MS). As he wrote in a subsequent letter to Comrade Pickles, opposing the sending of representatives to Parliament, 'tis no use prophesying as to the details of the revolution . . . if violence is inevitable, it will be begun by the reactionaries'(MS). The powers that be would not give up their position easily. In the book, once the war was over, society fairly rapidly became peaceful, a world in which all lived in pleasant places – the dream of the English and others of a quiet existence, where sordidness had been eliminated, as well as wealth and poverty. Equality had been achieved. The world is very much as if Morris & Co. had designed everything, and the inhabitants have learned Morris's lesson that pleasure in work results in more beautiful objects. Machines are at a minimum.

Morris recognised that these achievements had a price, though it was one that he was more than willing to pay. The atmosphere of this new society is non-intellectual, perhaps even anti-intellectual; reading does not appear to be central in most people's lives and they are leading a healthy, outdoor life; yet, as children, they learned how to read early – as Morris did – and picked up Latin and Greek.

There is no formal education. The country, nature, will ensure a happy life. So the trip from the city Kelmscott to the country Kelmscott emphasises the importance of a rural utopia. The book ends in a feast to celebrate the haymaking at the small Kelmscott church, now a banqueting hall; it is at that point at which the narrator fades, perhaps because he had never learned how to wield a scythe, and finds himself returned to 'dingy Hammersmith'. The illustrator, C. M.

Gere, in the Kelmscott Press edition of 1892, captured Morris's intense feeling for Kelmscott Manor in his drawing of the house, surrounded by a border designed by Morris, and the legend beneath it: 'This is the picture of the old house by the Thames to which the people of this story went.' (This provides a nice example of life imitating art; in the recent preservation of the Manor, the front door was changed to conform with the illustration.)

The notion of 'an epoch of rest' is applied in some degree to work itself. There is a little cutting of hay; there are people in attendance in shops; other tasks are suggested, but work is somewhat at a minimum. In this, Morris was prophetic of the present emphasis on the importance of leisure – the true values of life may be found in it rather than in work. The last line of the book asserts the potential reality of what he has written: 'If others can see it as I have seen it, then it may be called a vision rather than a dream.'

That he thought his picture of England no mere fantasy is indicated in a recently rediscovered lecture he gave in 1889. There, Morris emphasises his dedication to eliminating the division of labour, and alienation from labour, in a manner consistent with his own and with Marx's analyses:

We may have in appearance to give up a great deal of what we have been used to call material progress, in order that we may be freer, happier and more completely equal . . . This would be compensated (a) by our taking pleasurable interest in all the details of life, and (b) by our regaining the pleasure of the eyesight, much of which we have already lost, and more of which we are losing everyday . . . Work . . . obviously useful, and also adapted to the capacity of the worker would mostly be a pleasant exercise of the faculties; necessary work that would otherwise be drudgery would be done by machinery or in short spells: no one being condemned to work at unpleasant work all his life . . . [we will] do our best to remain men, even if in the struggle we become barbarians; which latter fate I must confess would not seem to me a very dreadful one.

Certainly the book's values – turning away from 'useless toil' to 'useful work', living more with the senses, cherishing nature and the land – mean more to many now than they may have done some years ago.

News from Nowhere shows a world in which life has been simplified. The Thames and its banks have been restored to an earlier beauty. Life has a medieval quality to it without the disadvantages of that hierarchical society. Art has come into what Morris regards as its own. Old Hammond tells Guest about the changes in society:

When men began to settle down after the war, and their labour had pretty much filled up the gap in wealth caused by the destruction of that war, a kind of disappointment seemed coming over us, and the prophecies of some of the reactionists of past times seemed as if they would come true, and a dull level of utilitarian comfort be the end for a while of our aspirations and success . . . Probably, from what I have told you before, you will have a guess at the remedy for such a disaster: remembering always that many of the things which used to be produced – slave-wares for the poor and more wealth-wasting wares for the rich – ceased to be made. That remedy was, in short, the production of what used to be called art, but which has no name amongst us now, because it has become a necessary part of the labour of every man who produces . . . The art or work-pleasure, as one ought to call it, of which I am now speaking, sprung up almost spontaneously, it seems from a kind of instinct amongst people, no longer driven desperately to painful and terrible overwork, to do the best they could with the work in hand – to make it excellent of its kind; and when they had gone on a little, a craving for beauty seemed to awaken in men's minds, and they began rudely and awkwardly to ornament the wares which they made; and when they had once set to work at that, it soon began to grow. All this was much helped by the abolition of the squalor which our immediate ancestors put up with so coolly; and by the leisurely, but not stupid, country-life which now grew . . . to be common amongst us. Thus at last and by slow degrees we got pleasure into our work; then we became conscious of that pleasure, and cultivated it, and took care that we had our fill of it; and then all was gained, and we were happy. So may it be for ages and ages! (Ch. XVIII)

This would seem to sum up what was perhaps the major theme of Morris's life. His ideal was that art and life should be inseparable. Despite his own success and his possible artistic influence, he felt that only with a socialist revolution could there be a permanent improvement in the status of art. As he wrote in 1883, the year he became a socialist, in his long autobiographical letter to Andreas Scheu:

I have not failed to be conscious that the art I have been helping to produce would fall with the death of a few of us who really care about it, that a reform in art which is founded on individualism must perish with the individuals who have set it going. Both my historical studies and my practical conflict with the philistinism of modern society have forced on me the conviction that art cannot have a real life and growth under the present system of commercialism and profit-mongering. I have tried to develop this view, which is in fact Socialism seen through the eyes of an artist, in various lectures, the first of which I delivered in 1878. (H 187)

The connected art and life of his utopian society were both beautiful and useful, without the price paid in medieval times of

violence, superstition, ignorance, slavery; yet I cannot help thinking that sorely as poor folks need a solace, they did not altogether lack one, and that solace was pleasure in their work . . . We must turn this land from the grimy back-yard of a workshop into a garden. If that seems difficult, or rather impossible, to some of you, I cannot help it; I only know that it is necessary. (CW XXII 163, 173)

Art was to be a democratic commodity, available to and made for all, 'a joy to the maker and the user'. In 'How I Became a

Socialist', the essay written in 1894, two years before his death, Morris summed up the impetus behind his vision:

Apart from the desire to produce beautiful things, the leading passion of my life has been and is hatred of modern civilisation . . . What shall I say concerning its mastery of, and its waste of mechanical power, its commonwealth so poor, its enemies of the commonwealth so rich, its stupendous organisation – for the misery of life . . . Its eyeless vulgarity which has destroyed art, the one certain solace of labour? . . . It must be remembered that civilisation has reduced the workman to such a skinny and pitiful existence, that he scarcely knows how to form a desire for any life much better than that which he now endures perforce. It is the province of art to set the true ideal of a full and reasonable life before him, a life to which the perception and creation of beauty, the enjoyment of real pleasure that is, shall be felt to be as necessary to man as his daily bread. (CW XXIII 279-81)

It was this state that had been achieved in *News from Nowhere*.

That book was undoubtedly Morris's most important publication in these years; but he also had an extraordinary further outburst of writing, mostly prose, but some poetry, in the so-called prose romances, tales of quest and adventure. In some respects *A Dream of John Ball* and *News from Nowhere* were part of this tradition, but they were explicitly political.

Between 1888 and his death in 1896 he published six of these books – *The House of the Wolfings* (1889). *The Roots of the Mountains* (1890), *The Story of the Glittering Plain* (1890), *The Wood beyond the Plain* (1890), *The Wood beyond the World* (1894), *Child Christopher* (1895), *The Well at the World's End* (1896). Two were published after his death, *The Water of the Wondrous Isles* (1897) and *The Story of the Sundering Flood* (1898). These romances were set elsewhere in time, in most cases in a somewhat mythological past. Until recently they tended to be the least regarded of Morris's writings, having dated, it was thought, even more than *The Earthly Paradise*, a

81

similarly fantastic tale. Their utopian elements are further-
more clearly connected with Morris's increased commitment
to politics and social change, although he himself vehemently
denied that the stories had any political significance. In 1895 a
reviewer in the *Spectator* claimed that *The Wood beyond the
World* was an allegory concerning Capital and Labour.
Morris felt constrained to reply: 'I had not the least intention
of thrusting an allegory into *The Wood beyond the World*: it is
meant for a tale pure and simple, with nothing didactic about
it. If I have to write or speak on social problems, I always try to
be as direct as I possibly can be' (H 371). He perhaps did not
wish to see that the depiction of another society whose more
primitive and non-capitalistic aspects help create a better
world does inevitably have political significance.

The writing of these tales – taking place in the world of
dreams and fairy tales – gave Morris pleasure, and they have
given pleasure to readers since – probably more so in recent
years than in the past. They are now reprinted in popular paperback editions, attracting those who enjoy the stories of Tolkien
and C. S. Lewis. In *The House of the Wolfings* and *The Roots of the
Mountains* Morris emphasised the importance of the tribe, as
opposed to the individual, seeing in it some sort of equiva-
lent – in both its strengths and its weaknesses – of a socialist
state. In these two books in particular, Morris dwelt on the virtues of Teutonic direct democracy and the vitality of German
barbarism, the qualities of fellowship and community. As they
were written when Morris was still at his most active politically,
it is not surprising that, whatever he might say, they should be
more explicitly political than the later romances. Morris
described *The House of the Wolfings* as 'the story of the Gothic
tribes on their way through Middle Europe, and their first
meeting with the Romans in war. It is meant to illustrate the
melting of the individual into the society of the tribes: I mean

apart from the artistic side of things that is its moral – if it has one' (H 302). Yet at the same time the stories tell of quests, of fulfilment, of awakening sexuality. As one commentator has remarked, 'All of the later prose romances pose questions of personal behavior and relationships in a background of commitment to some group of friends or some social community or kindred. Only when the personal relationships are resolved within the community can the story come to an end.' In these books, as in *News from Nowhere*, he is projecting an ideal society free of the vices of sordidness, human greed, and corruption. The prose romances were part of his quest for a better world.

The last eight years of Morris's life were dominated by books – those that he wrote, but even more so by those that he printed at the Kelmscott Press. In fact, the two interests sometimes came together, as when he rewrote the end of *Child Christopher* so that it would look better on the printed page. His interest in printing started when he was still intensely active in the political sphere, in 1888. At the time of the first show of the newly founded Arts & Crafts Exhibition Society, Morris was irritated to discover that no books of his own were worthy of being included. *The House of the Wolfings* was just in the process of being printed, and he took intense interest in that, advised by his artistic and political follower, Emery Walker. *The House of the Wolfings* was done in a special type modelled on an old Basel font, and with a feel for the proportion of the margins, and extra care was taken with the look of the title pages. The second romance – *The Roots of the Mountain* – was printed with changes that heralded the methods of the Kelmscott Press. Morris felt that it was the best-looking book produced since the seventeenth century. As with all that he did, the object was to make life better. He recognised that his activities in the world of design and literature were not really accessible to the ordinary person. He realised that such a person was too downtrodden to worry about the fine things in life. Nevertheless it was essential to set standards: 'To enjoy good houses and good books in self respect and decent comfort, seems to me to be the pleasurable end towards which all societies of human beings ought now to struggle.'

In connection with the first Arts & Crafts Exhibition in 1888, there was a series of lectures by various eminent figures. Morris himself gave one on tapestry and carpet weaving. Emery Walker gave a talk on printing, reflecting some of the concerns which Morris and he had in designing *The House of the Wolfings*. (In the 1893 printing of the lectures in *Arts and Crafts Essays*, an expanded version of the lecture is given as being by them both.) Walker dwelt on the necessity 'to have harmony between the type and the decoration', as Oscar Wilde reported the talk in the *Pall Mall Gazette*. For Morris the most important aspect was the projection of enlarged photographs of Jenson letters from the edition of Pliny on a screen: this inspired him with the possibility of designing type.

Morris has left a vivid account of the occasion in a letter to his daughter, Jenny, which also suggests the extraordinary pace of his activities:

I spoke on four consecutive days: last Saturday in St. Paul's Coffee, Sunday Hyde Park, Mondy [*sic*] Store St. Hall, Tuesday Clerkenwell Green. At the latter place there was a bit of a shindy but not till when I had gone away: as a result I had to bail a comrade on Wednesday and spend a couple of hours in that sink of iniquity a Police Court. Thursday I was at the Arts & Crafts at Walker's Lecture on printing: he was very nervous and ought to have written down his words; but of course he knew his subject thoroughly well: there were magic-lantern slides of pages of books, and some telling contrasts between the good and the bad. There was a ridiculous Yankee there who was very much 'risen' by Walker's attacks on the ugly American printing; who after the lecture came blustering up to Walker to tell him he was all wrong; so I went for him and gave him some candid speech on the subject of the said American periodicals. (H 303)

From then on one of the central activities in Morris's life was the creation of a Private Press. At the time such enterprises were comparatively rare; the greatest impetus to their rapid increase came from Morris. In December 1889, Morris asked Walker to go into partnership with him. Walker was too modest to accept, but he continued to advise Morris, finding him Joseph Batchelor as his papermaker, Edward Prince as his punch-cutter, Jaenecke of Hanover as the best producer of ink. Walker also produced enlarged photographs of letters which assisted Morris in designing type, the two that were used for most of the Kelmscott books: Golden and Troy.

The very last book published by the Kelmscott Press was *A Note by William Morris on His Aims in Founding the Kelmscott Press*, in 1898, two years after his death. In it, Morris wrote:

I began printing books with the hope of producing some which would have a definite claim to beauty, while at the same time they should be easy to read and should not dazzle the eye, or trouble the intellect of the reader by eccentricity of form in the letters. I have always been a great admirer of the calligraphy of the Middle Ages, of the earlier printing which took its place. As to fifteenth-century books, I had noticed that they were always beautiful by force of the mere typography, even without the added ornament, with which many of them are so lavishly supplied. And it was the essence of my undertaking to produce books which it would be a pleasure to look upon as pieces of printing and arrangement of type. Looking at my adventure from this point of view, then, I found I had to consider chiefly the following things: the paper, the form of the type, the relative spacing of the letters, the words, and the lines; and lastly the position of the printed matter on the page.

Thus began his 'little typographical adventure'. He was still very much interested in calligraphy, and as a dedicated medievalist he regarded it as superior to printing. But he was determined to create the best thought-out and most beautiful books that he could. His interest in printing and the writing of the prose romances have been frequently cited as indications of his disillusion with socialist politics. Clearly, there was some shift of interest and slowing down, although he retained his intense political commitment.

His split with the Socialist League made it financially easier for Morris to launch the Press: the money that he had been using to subsidise *Commonweal* could now be dedicated to his new endeavour. Also, the printer for that paper, Thomas Binning, became his chief pressman. He established the Press in Sussex House, opposite a pub called The Doves which gave its name to the Doves bindery of Thomas Cobden-Sanderson, and ultimately to the great private press established by Cobden-Sanderson and Emery Walker: The Doves Press. The Kelmscott Press issued its first book in the spring of 1891, *The Story of the Glittering Plain*. This version was unillustrated; it was reissued as the twenty-second book of the Press in 1894, with illustrations by Walter Crane. In total the Press published 53 books, three after Morris's death. Several were by Morris or translated by him, including eight volumes of *The Earthly Paradise*, as one title; then there were poems by Rossetti, Keats, Swinburne, Tennyson, Shakespeare, Shelley and Coleridge, More's *Utopia*, seventeen medieval texts, and various other books in which Morris was particularly interested. Here was a summation of many of the concerns of his life.

The masterpiece and most ambitious book of the Press was the folio Kelmscott Chaucer. The collected poems of one of Morris's hero figures, it had 87 woodcut illustrations by Burne-Jones. It took four years to produce. Though listed as the fortieth book for the Press, it was not finished until June 1896. Morris himself designed the decorative aspects of the book, such as initial words and borders. (He had made 644 designs for the Press during its existence.) Four hundred and twenty-five copies were printed on paper and thirteen on vellum. The former sold for £20, the latter for £120. But most of the Kelmscott Press books were quite reasonable in price. Morris attempted to create books which, although new in design, would suggest the quality of older books. The Press was similar to all his other enterprises in providing a sense of what was worth preserving as well as charting a course for the future. The Kelmscott Press was the progenitor of the other great private presses of the period: not only Doves, but Vale, Eragny, Ashendene, Essex House and others.

Though limited, items made by the Firm and the Press had a profound effect on the look of objects and books in wider production. The man who had considerable doubts about machines in fact was a major influence in improving the quality of what was produced by them. Perhaps there was some aspect of self-indulgence in the Press. Morris himself felt that such activities were merely palliative, considering the general rottenness of society. But as society has not transformed itself as he wished, we should be immensely grateful for the important, innovative and influential work he did through the Firm and the Press. The Press helped create a far greater concern for a beautiful page, and through the Arts & Crafts movement and art and printing schools Morris's influence spread throughout England and the world.

Towards the end of his life Morris renewed an interest which had perhaps an element of legitimate self-indulgence, of luxury. He began to collect books again, a hobby he had more or less abandoned in the early 1880s, although apparently it is not true, as had been believed, that he sold his collection in order to benefit the Democratic Federation. That was not necessary, as his annual income was £1,800 at this time. But in the 1890s he

returned to collecting early printed books and medieval illumi-
nated manuscripts. He was particularly fond of Gothic wood-
cuts. In 1895 he was buying at a great rate – for instance, a
thirteenth-century Book of Hours for £450, a fourteenth-
century *Roman de la Rose* for £400, a large folio French
thirteenth-century Bible for £650. Up until the end, he continued the pursuit – and surrounded himself with beautiful
books and manuscripts both from the past and of his own making. It was almost as if he were seeking a return for the beauty that
he had attempted to bring into the world.

Morris had been ill for more than a year before his death in
October 1896, but a serious decline was brought on by the complications of a cold caught in December 1895. He had been
speaking outside Waterloo station as part of the funeral for his
old friend, Sergius Stepniak, the Russian revolutionary, who
had been run down by a train while absent-mindedly crossing
the tracks in Chiswick. Morris went on a cruise to Norway, he
worked on Kelmscott Press books, he continued to write, but he
was clearly failing. It was a sad, protracted death. In September,
Arnold Dolmetsch, who had done so much to recover older
music and instruments, played the virginals for him. Morris
died on 3 October at 11:15, and was buried in the village of
Kelmscott on 6 October. The funeral was appropriately simple,
yet dramatic: a very wet day, a howling wind, the rising waters of
the Thames, the coffin carried in an open hay cart, a wreath of
bay, a simple service in the church, the mourners being the vil-
lagers, friends, workers from Merton Abbey, quite a few members of the Art Workers' Guild. The family remained at
Kelmscott Manor, and after May Morris's death the house
went first to Oxford University and then to the Society of
Antiquaries. Philip Webb built a gravestone for him, raised
from the ground on short stone stilts, in the face of the minister's
objections to such an unconventional tomb. Even in death,

Morris did things differently. As Webb wrote to Jane Morris, 'If I could put a semblance of a roof over him, in mimic show of an Iceland one, it would not vex him if his spirit was alight there under it; like that of one of his old northern heroes in his cairn' (MS).

I hope that the preceding pages have made clear how extensive were Morris's ideas. He influenced so wide an area – in design, as a writer, as a socialist – that it is possible to see his life as hopelessly diffused. But in fact there is, I believe, a strong consistent line in his thought. He wished to reform the world, to simplify life, to make it more rewarding, to make it more beautiful, to make it more just, to make the joy of it available to more and more people, to fight against shoddy, to remove 'mumbo-jumbo' from the world. These conceptions are stronger for us because of his ideas: he was central in changing our vision of the world. He did not accomplish all that he hoped, but it is astounding how much he did.

'Have nothing in your houses that you do not know to be useful, or believe to be beautiful.' Morris's views on the environment, on preserving what is of value in both the natural and the 'built' worlds, on decentralising bloated government, are as significant now as they were in Morris's own time, or even more so. Earlier in the twentieth century much of his thinking, particularly its political side, was dismissed as sheer romanticism. After the Second World War, it appeared that modernisation, centralisation, industrialism, rationalisation – all the faceless movements of the time – were in control and would take care of the world. Today, when we have a keen sense of the shambles of their efforts, the suggestions which Morris made in his designs, his writings, his actions and his politics have new power and relevance.

Further Reading

Writings by Morris

Books by and about William Morris are legion, although they are harder to come by than one might think, as not very much is in print. The standard collection is in twenty-four volumes, *The Collected Works*, edited by his daughter, May (Longmans Green, London, 1910–15), supplemented by two further volumes also edited by her, *William Morris Artist, Writer, Socialist* (Blackwell, Oxford, 1936, reissued, Russell & Russell, New York, 1966). Philip Henderson has edited *The Letters of William Morris to His Family and Friends* (London, 1950).

Various of Morris's works have been available in paperback editions. Geoffrey Grigson, ed., with an introduction, *A Choice of William Morris's Verse* (Faber and Faber, London, 1969); Asa Briggs, ed., *William Morris Selected Writings and Designs* (Penguin Books, Harmondsworth, 1962), A. L. Morton, ed., *Three Works by William Morris: News from Nowhere, The Pilgrims of Hope, A Dream of John Ball* (International Publishers, New York, 1968); A. L. Morton, ed., *Political Writings of William Morris* (International Publishers, New York, 1973); Robert W. Gutman, ed., *Volsunga Saga* (Collier, New York, 1962). The renewed interest in works of fantasy has resulted in paperbacks of some of the prose romances, such as Lin Carter, ed., *The Sundering Flood* and *The Well at the World's End* (Ballantine Books, New York, 1973 and 1975); Tom Shippey, ed., *The Wood Beyond the World* (Oxford University Press, 1980).

Writings about Morris

There are numerous biographies and short studies, of which the authorised biography in two volumes is by Edward Burne-Jones's son-in-law, J. W. Mackail, *The Life of William Morris* (Longmans Green, London, 1899, reissued, Benjamin Blom, New York, 1968).

The four major largely biographical studies of recent years are E. P. Thompson, *William Morris: Romantic to Revolutionary* (Merlin Press, London, 1955, revised edition, 1977); Paul Thompson, *The Work of William Morris* (The Viking Press, New York, 1967, reissued, 1977); Philip Henderson, *William Morris* (McGraw-Hill, New York, 1967); Jack Lindsay, *William Morris* (Constable, London, 1975). Two recent shorter studies are Ian Bradley, *William Morris and His World* (Charles Scribner's Sons, New York, 1978), heavily illustrated, and Peter Faulkner, *Against the Age: An Introduction to William Morris* (George Allen & Unwin, London, 1980).

Design: A general study is Ray Watkinson, *William Morris as Designer* (Reinhold Corporation, New York, 1967, new edition, 1979). Two broad studies put Morris's design work in perspective: Gillian Naylor, *The Arts and Crafts Movement* (Studio Vista, London, 1971), and Nikolaus Pevsner, *Pioneers of Modern Design, From William Morris to Walter Gropius* (Penguin Books, Harmondsworth, 3rd edition, 1970). The interpretation implied by the subtitle is controversial in its argument concerning Morris's role in the creation of modern architecture.

Architecture and Artefacts

Many British museums contain objects manufactured by William Morris, most notably the Victoria and Albert Museum in London which also houses the Green Dining Room done by the Firm, as well as textiles that Morris studied and helped select. There is the William Morris Gallery itself in Walthamstow, London. Three of Morris's houses are open at times to the public: The Red House in Bexleyheath, Kent, privately owned, Kelmscott Manor, Kelmscott, Gloucestershire, belonging to the Society of Antiquaries, and Kelmscott House, Upper Mall, Hammersmith, London, owned by the William Morris Society.

Index

Index

Past Masters

GEORGE ELIOT Rosemary Ashton

This book shows how Mary Ann Evans, translator, witty reviewer and editor in all but name of the radical *Westminster Review*, evolved into George Eliot, a great novelist who applied her tolerant philosophy of humanity and comic wit to the imaginative re-creation of English society. Rosemary Ashton demonstrates the influence of Spinoza, Goethe and Feuerbach on George Eliot's thinking, and explores her view of the novelist's task as that of the 'natural historian' of society.

COLERIDGE Richard Holmes

Coleridge was not only a great poet, he was also a philosopher and explorer of the whole human condition. Richard Holmes describes Coleridge's work as a writer, explains his often difficult and fragmentary ideas, and shows that his concept of the creative imagination still shapes our notions of growth and culture.

'most attractive' *Listener*

'stylish, intelligent and readable' *Irish Times*

NEWMAN Owen Chadwick

The religious leader John Henry Newman started his long career as a devout Protestant; he later became the head of a new movement of Catholic ideas within the Church of England, and finally joined the Roman Catholic Church. He began a new epoch in the study of religious faith. Professor Chadwick examines the many aspects of Newman's thought and writings, especially his views about faith, knowledge and education.

'a fine introduction to the spirit of Newman' *Sunday Times*

Past Masters

MARX Peter Singer

Peter Singer identifies the central vision that unifies Marx's thought, enabling us to grasp Marx's views as a whole. He views him as a philosopher primarily concerned with human freedom, rather than as an economist or social scientist. He explains alienation, historical materialism, the economic theory of *Capital*, and Marx's idea of communism, in plain English, and concludes with a balanced assessment of Marx's achievement.

'an admirably balanced portrait of the man and his achievement'
Observer

ENGELS Terrell Carver

In a sense, Engels invented Marxism. His chief intellectual legacy, the materialist interpretation of history, has had a revolutionary effect on the arts and social sciences, and his work as a whole did more than Marx's to make converts to the most influential political movement of modern times. In this book Terrell Carver traces Engels's career, and looks at the effect of the materialist interpretation of history on Marxist theory and practice.

'Carver's refreshingly honest book . . . is packed with careful judgements about the different contributions of Engels to 19th century marxism.' *New Society*

DARWIN Jonathan Howard

Darwin's theory that men's ancestors were apes caused a furore in the scientific world and outside it when *The Origin of Species* was published in 1859. Arguments still rage about the implications of his evolutionary theory, and scepticism about the value of Darwin's contribution to knowledge is widespread. In this analysis of Darwin's major insights and arguments, Jonathan Howard reasserts the importance of Darwin's work for the development of modern biology.

'Jonathan Howard has produced an intellectual *tour de force*, a classic in the genre of popular scientific exposition which will still be read in fifty years' time.' *Times Literary Supplement*

Past Masters

CARLYLE A. L. Le Quesne

A. L. Le Quesne examines the views of this first and most influential of the Victorian 'prophets', explaining how his greatness lay in his ability to voice the needs of a remarkably moral generation.

'A first-rate introduction . . . it is not the least of the merits of this excellent short study that it shows some of the tensions yet to be found in reading Carlyle.' *Edinburgh University Journal*

TOLSTOY Henry Gifford

This book is primarily concerned with Tolstoy's thought, as expressed both in his fiction and didactic writings. Henry Gifford sets his subject in the context of nineteenth-century Russia and Europe, and shows how Tolstoy's life expressed the aspirations and perplexities of his country in a gathering crisis.

'Within its brief span . . . the reader is told, in a graceful, informative manner, about Tolstoy's life and times and about the meaning of his major writings . . . The book is, in the best sense, a job of cultural mediation.' *Times Literary Supplement*

PROUST Derwent May

Marcel Proust's great novel, *Remembrance of Things Past*, is not only an epic work of lyrical reminiscence, it is also a dazzling and witty portrait of French character and society. Derwent May explores the historical and social aspects of Proust's novel, and examines the relationship between Proust's ideas and those of the narrator of the book, Marcel, particularly emphasising the way in which the book's style reflects its content.

'A delightful little introduction and celebration of one of the great books of our century.' *The Times*

Past Masters

THE BUDDHA Michael Carrithers

Michael Carrithers guides us through the complex and sometimes conflicting information that Buddhist texts give about the life and teaching of the Buddha. He discusses the social and political background of India in the Buddha's time, and traces the development of his thought. He also assesses the rapid and widespread assimilation of Buddhism, and its contemporary relevance.

MUHAMMAD Michael Cook

Just over a sixth of the world's population subscribes to the Muslim belief that 'there is no god but God, and Muhammad is His Messenger'. Michael Cook gives an incisive account of the man who inspired this faith, drawing on the traditional Muslim sources to describe Muhammad's life and teaching. He also attempts to stand back from this traditional picture to question how far it is historically justified.